Also by Darlene Powell Hopson, Ph.D.,
and Derek S. Hopson, Ph.D.

Different and Wonderful

Raising the Rainbow Generation

Teaching Your Children to Be Successful in a Multicultural Society

by

Darlene Powell Hopson, Ph.D.,
and Derek S. Hopson, Ph.D.,

with

Thomas Clavin

A FIRESIDE BOOK • Published by Simon & Schuster
New York London Toronto Sydney Tokyo Singapore

F

FIRESIDE
Rockefeller Center
1230 Avenue of the Americas
New York, New York 10020

FIRESIDE and colophon are registered trademarks of
Simon & Schuster Inc.

Designed by Crowded House Design
Manufactured in the United States of America

10   9   8   7   6   5   4   3   2   1

Library of Congress Cataloging-in-Publication Data
Hopson, Darlene Powell.
    Raising the rainbow generation : teaching your children to be successful in
a multicultural society / by Darlene Powell Hopson and Derek S. Hopson
with Thomas Clavin.
        p.   cm.
    "A Fireside book."
    Includes bibliographical references and index.
    1. Prejudices in children—United States—Prevention.   2. Race
awareness in children—United States.   3. Multiculturalism—United
States.   4. Child rearing—United States.   I. Hopson, Derek S.
II. Clavin, Thomas.   III. Title.
BF723.P75H67   1993
649'.1—dc20   93-28075   CIP
ISBN 0-671-79806-5

Acknowledgments

We are especially grateful to Sydny Miner and Marilyn Abraham at Simon & Schuster for their encouragement, unceasing patience, constant courtesy, and for being wonderful editors. We also want to thank our agent, Barbara Lowenstein, for helping to make our dream come true.

During the preparation and writing of this book we received assistance from many expert sources and support from friends and family. Without them, *Raising the Rainbow Generation* wouldn't have been possible. If this book contributes to helping our children to create a stronger society for their children, it's because we were inspired by them and other people of all colors who demonstrate every day that we can live together.

This book is dedicated to all of our children,
Derek & Darlene's
Dotteanna Hopson
Derek S. Hopson, Jr.
Tom & Nancy's
Kathryn Clavin
Brendan Clavin
and to all of your children.

Contents

10   Contents

Introduction

We didn't choose to write this book. It chose us.

In the late spring of 1990, we received a call from Tom Clavin, who interviewed us for an article he was writing for *Child* magazine on the subtle messages parents send children that reveal their racial attitudes. This began a series of events that told us this book needed to be written and that we should do it.

One event was the publication that year of our first book, *Different and Wonderful: Raising Black Children in a Race-Conscious Society.* Though, as the title indicates, this book was directed at black parents, we received calls from and were approached by people of all races who wanted to know how their children or students could learn to live together and appreciate diversity. During our book tour and in our private practice, we heard this concern over and over.

We began the process of thinking about this book, collecting materials, and talking to colleagues and friends. And nearly every day we read a newspaper article or saw a TV news report on the increase of racially motivated crimes. We realized that children were being exposed to overt and covert messages that people of different races and cultures could not get along.

Another event was the response to the *Child* magazine article. There were many letters to the editor, most of them from white parents, asking the same questions: "What do we do? How do we raise children who will not be afraid of people with different skin colors?" It was obvious to us that there was an eagerness across the country to produce a new generation that would at the very least not have the fear, mistrust, and suspicions that previous generations had. There had to be a way to tap the energy of those good intentions.

A third factor was the discussions we and Tom had over several months. He and his wife, Nancy, had two young children, and we had a young daughter (our son was born in September 1992), so as parents we were concerned about preparing our children to live in a society more racially and culturally diverse than at any time before. Here we were, black people and white people, trying to figure out how our children—and by extension all children of all colors—could be friends.

This sounded like a good idea for a book, and we set to work. Our professional experience was very helpful, particularly a project we had done in 1985 based on a study conducted by Drs. Kenneth and Mamie Clark in the late 1930s and early 1940s. That study used dolls to document the impact of negative racial images on black children. The Clarks asked youngsters to choose between black and white dolls on the basis of which one they identified with. Sixty-seven percent of black preschool children chose the white dolls.

In our study, we repeated and expanded on the doll tests, asking questions of both black and white youngsters. Not only did 65 percent of black children choose the white dolls (only a 2 percent decrease after almost fifty years!), but 76 percent of the black children and 82 percent of the white children said that the black dolls "looked bad" to them.

The responses of the black children led to our first book. Yet lingering in our minds was the response of the white youngsters. Their view of the black dolls was probably only the tip of the iceberg, and other negative views were likely present. We extended this thought to suppose that, whether a child is black, white, brown, yellow, or red, he or she is growing up with a negative or uninformed outlook toward people of other races.

This was a distressing thought. At the same time as America was becoming even more multiracial, there was no progress in understanding and appreciation between races and cultures. As professionals we could simply continue to study the situation. But as people who believe in the ideal of peaceful coexistence, and especially as parents, we had to get involved.

Working on the proposal for the book we intended to write seemed like a positive action. The experience of writing our first book had been rewarding, and we enjoyed the prospect of writing another. And in Tom we found a willing and equally concerned collaborator. But then something else happened, something that gave us a sense of urgency that this new book must be written.

We had nearly completed the proposal when Los Angeles exploded. In the spring of 1991, we and millions of other people watched the reports on TV of whites, blacks, Asians, and Latinos battling among themselves, the violence fueled both by rage over the acquittal of four white police officers who had been charged with savagely beating a black motorist in that city and by the overwhelming hostility the groups had for one another. For a few frightening moments, we wondered if any attempt to foster understanding and bridge gaps was too late. And we received numerous calls from anxious parents asking, "Is this the legacy we're leaving for our children? Can't we find a way to get along?"

So in a sense this book chose us, because we firmly believe it's not too late to find ways to live together. What happened in Los Angeles and the incidents of racial conflict elsewhere in the country can be a preview of the society our children will come of age in. Or they can be an aberration, or, better yet, a blessing in disguise: These events will spur us into action so that they won't happen again.

Perhaps you've made your own beginning, in your home, school, and community. But if not, if you want to try yet aren't sure how, if you don't want to go it alone—we hope you'll use this book as a starting point.

That's why we had to write it. We want our children, Tom's children, the children of our friends and neighbors, *all children* to grow up rejecting prejudice, fear and hatred, and instead be open to the fascinating qualities people of every color and culture have to offer. Let's make this our legacy.

This book doesn't attempt to change society, or even your immediate environment, overnight. We show how in many small ways understanding can be promoted. The book contains anecdotes, discussions, exercises, and practical tips you can employ on an everyday basis.

We also discuss how, when, and why children acquire biased attitudes. Obviously, parents are the strongest influence, just as they are with anything a child learns. Please don't be alarmed if you think your influence has not been wholly positive. No parent is perfect. Focus more on the fact that by putting your good intentions into practice, you will produce results no one and nothing else could. Childhood is a time of exciting opportunities.

Other discussions deal with the influence of the schools, media, and peers, both yours and your child's. We cannot control everything a youngster is exposed to, but being aware of the power of other influences enables us to counteract negative influences and support positive ones.

We have also included a variety of folktales. Children are born curious, and over the years stories expand their horizons. Whether you read them to your child (or students) or they are old enough to read them themselves, the folktales offer views of other peoples and cultures. Selecting these stories from other countries emphasized to us that what we have in common is larger than our differences. We think reading them offers children the chance to appreciate other cultures and to incorporate the concept that many things—such as love of family, the quest for origins, the struggle for survival in an uncertain environment, developing intelligence, the value of friendship—are universal.

This book is for the parents, teachers, and other caregivers of children under age twelve. This doesn't mean you can't adapt some of its information to adolescents, but we've focused on younger children because they are the most impressionable. What they learn now—and they learn so fast!—lasts a lifetime. Think about it: Do we expect children to learn how to read and write, and acquire other important tools for living all by themselves? Of course not. They are taught and they learn.

Learning to reject bias can happen now. Learning to appreciate the joys and mysteries of other cultures can happen now. Learning to be comfortable with curiosity about people with different skin color or facial features can happen now. And learning to celebrate diversity instead of to fear it can happen now.

It won't happen immediately. As you all know, child rearing is a long-term vocation, and the results of all our efforts may not be apparent for many years. But let's begin now, together.

—Darlene Powell Hopson and Derek Hopson

Part 1

Appreciation Begins at Home

1

Past Imperfect, Present Tense

Whenever someone asked us about this book and we told them what it was about, the response was usually, "What a great idea. We could use a book like this!" We were pleased to hear that people not only were interested in the subject but would put it to use in their homes and classrooms.

Yet one response was disturbing. After being given a brief description of the book over the phone, one caller said, "You could be wasting your time. Everybody has biases; you can't change that. And with kids, once they go out into the world they make up their own minds."

We don't disagree that, as youngsters experience more of the world around them, they form judgments. But the caller missed the point: We try as best we can to teach our children what we think is right and to have open minds so the judgments they form will be reasonable.

Too often children have little or no knowledge of people with different racial or ethnic backgrounds, or grow up fearing people different from themselves. Inevitably, their judgments are based on ignorance, anxiety, lack of personal contact, or fear. Our hope is that by fostering an appreciation of others, we can assist children to begin on the path toward acquiring attitudes and making decisions with an open mind.

Why is there a need to learn to respect and appreciate others, or at least live together peaceably? Of course, the need has always been there—very few, if any, societies throughout history were completely homogeneous, with all their citizens looking and talking the same way.

But the need is critical now because our society is changing. The America of the twenty-first century will be unlike the America of any previous century because its population will be racially and culturally diverse as never before.

In a speech to college students in November 1990, Dr. Belinda Ramirez, a member of the U.S. Commission on Civil Rights, said: "In the next generation America will become the most diverse pluralistic nation in the history of the world. Never before will we have such a situation of cultures living together under one democracy."

Dr. Ramirez added, however, that "the bottom line is we don't know how to become that pluralistic nation of the future. There are no models in history. We need to learn how to become that kind of society."

How accurate is her prediction? One way to determine this is to observe for ourselves. All around us, in just about every community, there are members of African American, Latino, Asian Pacific, and other groups in the classroom, in the workplace, on the same block, in the media. Compare this situation to when you were a child. Isn't it obvious the "melting pot" has become much more full and diverse?

How has our society come to be this diverse? It began in 1607, when settlers from England arrived in Virginia and there encountered the Powhatan Indians. Only twelve years later—a year before the *Mayflower* dropped anchor off Plymouth Rock—the first Africans arrived, twenty men and women who had been abducted from a slave trader bound for the West Indies.

Two of them, Antony and Isabella, married; and in 1624 their son, Martin Tucker, became the first black child born in the colonies. There were now three races living side by side. It seems that 370 years later, we're still trying to figure out how to live together in peace.

With the exception of Native Americans, all of us are descended from immigrants. Before this century, the largest number of people arriving on these shores were Africans, brought against their will. By 1820, at least ten million slaves were shipped to the Americas, five times the number of immigrants from Europe. A large percentage of the Africans didn't survive. They died en route or perished in their new "home" from exposure to harsh physical and psychological conditions.

The ratio significantly changed after 1820. During the next century, over 90 percent of the thirty-six million immigrants to this country were from Europe—Germans, Italians, Irish, and Eastern Europeans. They had two distinct advantages over the Africans: They weren't slaves, though some served temporarily as indentured servants, and their physical appearance was not as different.

This book is not the place to discuss the history of slavery, but we would like to make one point: Slavery indelibly stamped into the American consciousness the belief that blacks were inferior. No European group was ever enslaved in America. For slavery to endure as an institution to 1863, it was essential that society consider black people as less than human. Even as slavery became illegal, numerous laws were enacted to promote, or at least condone, racism and to deny blacks a share of the American Dream.

And the American Indians, as we know, became outcasts in their own land, killed or pushed farther west until the population was threatened with extinction.

Ironically, in this century any respite from racism for blacks has been due to the fact that racism has been spread around a bit more. More-recent immigrants have been from Latino, Asian Pacific, and Middle Eastern countries. They too have different physical appearances, which to some extent leads to the belief that they also are inferior.

Now let's try to put into perspective how society has changed and is changing at a more rapid rate, which makes clear the need to prepare the next generation for a racial and cultural climate never before experienced in America.

Even if you still live in a neighborhood that is all or predominantly one color, please consider these statistics:

• By the end of this decade, less than half the students in California will be of European origin.
• In 1992, 26 percent of the homes and apartments purchased in New York City, Westchester County, the seven counties in northern New Jersey and on Long Island were bought by people who had been born outside the U.S.
• Also in 1992, the New York City public school system had twenty thousand more students enroll than in the previous year. The system

now has its highest enrollment in fourteen years, with students representing 167 countries. The bulk of the new enrollment are youngsters from the Caribbean, the Dominican Republic, and Jamaica.

• In the Boston area, four out of every ten residents are members of minority groups. It is projected that, in the city, white residents will be the minority by the year 2000.

• Less-populated areas are changing, too. In New Hampshire, for example, in the last six years the percentage of nonwhite students has quintupled.

• Many colleges are experiencing leaps in the enrollment of minority students. At the University of California at Berkeley, the minority population has gone from 34 to 55 percent.

• Cities, of course, are seeing the widest range of diversity. But according to the 1990 U.S. census, in the previous decade Connecticut's black population doubled, and in the five suburban counties surrounding New York City there was an increase of 285,000 Asian Pacific, Latino, and black residents.

• The census also found that in the last decade there has been a 52 percent increase in the number of Latino households. The impact on the economy has already been felt. Latino buying power, the census determined, has leaped 67 percent.

• Nationwide, according to the census, there was a 45.1 percent jump in the number of people classified as "other race."

• A recent study by the U.S. Department of Labor projected that by the year 2050, 75 percent of this country's work force will be people of color. Also by the middle of the next century, the U.S. population will include eighty-two million people who arrived in this country after 1991 or were born of parents who did; this group will account for two out of every five people in America.

These changes are making news. A front-page story in the March 11, 1991, issue of the *New York Times* began:

The racial and ethnic complexion of the American population changed more dramatically in the past decade than at any time in the 20th century, with nearly one in every four Americans claiming African, Asian, Hispanic or American Indian ancestry. . . . In the field of population statistics, where change sometimes seems glacially slow, the speed at which the country's racial and ethnic mix was altered in the 1980s was breathtaking, Census figures show. The rate of increase in the minority population was nearly twice as fast as in the 1970s.

Unless there is an astonishing reversal, your child will truly be a part of a "rainbow generation" in twenty-first-century America. People of all backgrounds will be making our political decisions, running our economy, and creating our culture.

Unfortunately, the changes have inspired more conflict than tolerance. On almost a daily basis there are headlines proclaiming bias incidents, violent confrontations between individuals of different backgrounds. Most of them are based on racial differences: A black man walking down the street with a white woman is attacked by white youths; a fifteen-year-old girl is attacked by black assailants because she is "white and perfect"; in another community, stores owned by Koreans are vandalized or torched by white and black residents whose mistrust boiled over into action.

These statistics are startling and distressing:

• The National Institute Against Prejudice and Violence reports that one in five black students has experienced some form of racial harassment, and during a five-year period racist episodes have been reported at more than three hundred colleges and universities.
• In a recent Gallup poll designed to assess racial attitudes, done for *New York Newsday,* it was found that two out of every five whites in the region expressed one or more negative stereotypes about blacks.
• According to the U.S. Department of Justice's Community Relations Service, incidents of interracial conflict nationwide have leaped 31 percent since 1987. At the same time, the CRS says reports of "excessive use of force" by police in racial incidents have soared 39 percent.

Because of the tensions that are straining the fragile fabric of our society, we believe this book had to be written. To prepare its children for the future is the goal of every generation. For our children to thrive and have a chance to live in harmony, we must prepare them for a unique twenty-first-century America.

2
A Look Around and in the Mirror

Let's look around us for a minute. Why is tension between races so pervasive? Why do stereotypes persist? Why are we having so much trouble living together?

One reason why the so-called melting pot is simmering is the simple fact, as demographic statistics in the last chapter demonstrated, that there are so many people with so many diverse backgrounds. This situation is so new that we haven't quite got our bearings, and in uncertain situations people feel threatened.

Iowa has become one of eight states in the United States to enact an educational choice program for parents—they can decide which schools their children attend. In Des Moines, during the first two years of the program, 402 white students left the public school system, compared to only eleven students of color. Some of the parents admitted that this was a case of white flight: They feared the changing racial composition of the public schools.

In effect, those parents felt threatened. Instead of finding ways to deal with a new situation, they chose to get away from it.

Another reason for unrest is that some white people feel threatened by changing demographics. America in the twenty-first century will not be anything like what it's been for the last four centuries, when whites were clearly the dominant population and culture. Will they be overwhelmed? Will they be subjected to the discrimination previously practiced against minority groups?

One indication of the threat whites feel is that in the last few years the number of white-supremacist hate groups has significantly increased. According to Klanwatch, an organization based in Alabama, there are now 346 such groups, most of them found in Georgia, Florida, California, the Northeast Corridor, and Chicago.

A third reason for interracial tensions is the economy. Throughout American history, during times of economic distress Americans have turned more conservative. They see the pie shrinking and more people trying to cut a slice. People feel angry when they lose jobs, homes, and opportunities, and often that anger takes the form of blaming someone else. The most obvious targets are people different from ourselves, whether they be brown, yellow, black, or white. During the late 1980s and into the 1990s, the sluggish economy has fueled that feeling. Current psychology defines this dynamic as displacement. Here, the disappointment and frustration of everyday life are relieved by expressing anger and aggression toward what is perceived as an available target.

There has also been, to some extent, a backlash against affirmative action programs and civil rights legislation that began in the 1960s. Providing opportunities for all can mean not as many opportunities for some whose vistas were once unlimited.

Due to limited contact between racial groups, there is a lack of understanding or there is mistrust. In May 1992, *Time* magazine and CNN conducted a poll to assess how one group perceives another. Sixty-five percent of blacks surveyed believed whites thought they "have no self-discipline," but only 17 percent of whites actually said that; 63 percent rejected the idea. Though 75 percent of blacks believed whites thought them prone to crime, only 34 percent of whites said they had that belief.

There is additional misunderstanding of Latinos, who by the year 2013 will be the dominant "minority" group in the United States. Some people who harbor stereotypes about Latinos might be surprised to learn that, according to a study conducted in Southern California, Latinos have fewer low-birth-weight babies than whites, half as many Latinos as whites are on welfare, proportionately more Latino males are in the work force than whites, and Latino couples are half as likely to divorce as white couples.

To show how complicated and contradictory this matter of social perception and racial attitude is, during a similar period a social survey by the National Opinion Research Center found that most of those who responded believe in a "fair and equal" society. Yet the survey also found that whites retain negative stereotypes about blacks and Latinos. The majority of white respondents believe that people in those two groups are prone to violence, are less intelligent, are less hard-working, and prefer "living on welfare."

One other factor is that racism is deeply ingrained in the American psyche, with the attitude that if you're discriminated against, there's a good reason for it. Commenting on the high poverty and unemployment rates among nonwhite groups, Thomas Powell, author of *The Persistence of Racism in America*, wrote:

> *We cling to the notion that what people "deserve" usually decides what they get. If we are fairly pleased with our situations, we can enjoy them as reflections of our "inner qualities"—character, determination, perseverance, etc. Maybe even Yankee ingenuity and pioneer resourcefulness. So we think, or somehow feel, the false corollary that people who lead unenviable lives probably lack such "inherent" qualities.*

So it's okay to believe in stereotypes, because if they weren't true, we wouldn't have them. If we treat you as inferior, it must be because you *are* inferior.

Andrew Hacker, in *Two Nations: Black and White, Separate, Hostile, Unequal*, wrote:

> *The white virus afflicts virtually all white families in America. It breeds the belief that because we're white, we belong to a superior evolutionary strain, one that allows us to take certain privileges for granted. We—or most of us—also feel that this is "our" country, and that other groups of people, particularly those of African descent, are here on a kind of probation, at our sufferance. In other words, other races cannot be fully American. It's not easy for white parents to tell their children, "You are not superior to anyone," but it needs to be done.*

For many Americans, the events that comprised the Rodney King incident were jarring examples of the tension between races. King, a black man, was savagely beaten by four white police officers in 1991. A year later, those officers were acquitted of the beating by an all-white jury in a suburb of Los Angeles. Immediately afterward, the city was engulfed by violent strife. On TV sets we witnessed blacks and Latinos rioting, burning stores (especially those owned by Asians), and nearly beating a white truck driver to death.

Most of us were horrified. But what is also horrifying is that it could happen again, anywhere, perhaps in your community and certainly in any community in America that has not made a strong effort to bridge the gaps of resentment, mistrust, and fear between racial groups.

How do we bridge those gaps? Start with the children. No child is born biased. Children perceive the world based on influences, and those influences can prod them toward bigotry or toward an appreciation of others.

We don't advocate teaching respect for others because you *have* to do it. It's not like a business proposition, where your child will get a better deal in life by being able to interact with people of other groups (though we believe this is true). We fully realize that millions of American parents want to promote respect and appreciation simply because they believe it is the right thing to do. They either know or suspect that celebrating cultural differences will offer their children the opportunity to experience relationships outside their own race or ethnic group that are enjoyable, stimulating, and growth-enhancing. Life is far richer for all of us when we can understand and share ourselves with others.

But good intentions alone won't produce this satisfying result. There is work involved. And before we can start with the children, *you* have to begin.

On a recent Saturday one of the authors attended a workshop at a community college on Long Island (New York) for instructors of freshman-orientation courses. Of the several topics covered that day, Cultural Diversity provoked the most vocal participation.

Finally, the workshop organizers pleaded with the group of seventy or so people to move on to the next topic. Yet one woman stood up and said, "I think we all want to help our students and our children learn how to live together. But before we can help them, *we* have to look in the mirror and have a real honesty session with ourselves." This statement was greeted with loud applause.

Are you ready to take a look?

Most of us who are parents rarely look in the mirror. One reason is time. Though parenting is often a thrilling, satisfying experience, it is also hectic and exhausting. Caring for children can be like riding in a car with *them* at the wheel, increasing speed as they grow up, while we're holding on, hoping that our love and advice will help them steer in the right direction. Who has the time to pause to evaluate our performance?

Another reason is a certain amount of anxiety. If we take a good, hard look, there's a chance we won't like what we see. We're afraid that even by trying our best, we haven't turned out to be exactly the sort of parents we intended to be.

One issue that can fall by the wayside is our attitudes toward people of other races and how we might be communicating those attitudes to children. Let's face it: When we're involved in earning a living, providing adequate health care, maintaining a household, paying taxes, and monitoring the school curriculum, racial attitudes can seem less pressing.

Of course, some parents who do consider race relations important might not do anything about them. They can lack confidence or, being confused about the subject, think that it's better to do or say nothing than to make a mistake. Or they think, "We'll get around to it eventually."

Racial issues can be like sex, another topic parents are reluctant to introduce. If you have young children, can you actually say you are looking forward to the time when you will discuss sex with them? But there is an important difference between racial issues and sex. With the latter, you know the day will come when you have to provide an understanding of the birds and the bees, or otherwise risk a pregnancy or a sexually transmitted disease.

With racial issues, the day might never come (though your child *is* thinking about the topic), and ignorance of other races and cultures won't lead to pregnancy and disease. But by not getting involved, you are jeopardizing your child's healthy emotional development as well as impairing her ability to fully participate in society. The need to intervene in this subject is really no less urgent and shouldn't be postponed. Besides, racism is an emotional disease.

When do you think children begin to form attitudes about people with skin colors different from their own?

Many of us might say five or six or seven. Usually at these ages children verbalize their thoughts about people they might consider different or even strange. We think, "Ah, Vicky is curious about black (white, brown, yellow, red) people, so I guess it's time to talk to her."

Though it's not too late at this point, it is later than you think. Verbalizing at age five or seven doesn't mean curiosity has begun, only that the curiosity is being expressed.

Children become aware of racial differences at an early age. The most recent studies have concluded that children notice differences by age three, and many experts suspect future studies will reveal an even younger age of awareness.

At this age children also categorize; they can separate people by color. Obviously, input from a parent about a certain skin color can lead the child to form an attitude about that color and the person who wears it.

Think about it: At age three, even if your child is in nursery school, a day-care center, an informal play group—or even plopped in front of a TV—is there anyone other than *you* who will have a greater effect on the conclusions he or she is beginning to draw?

That's why it is essential that parents pause, take a deep breath, slip the phone off the hook, turn off the radio or TV . . . and look in the mirror. How *do* you feel about people of other races and cultures? And are you uncomfortable with the prospect that when your children are older, they will exist side by side with people of other racial groups to an extent never seen before in this society?

Okay, you're looking in the mirror. What if you don't like everything you see? (And we don't mean your clothes, your thighs, or your receding hairline.) What if you see within yourself some degree of fear, mistrust, even dislike?

Please don't feel you have already failed and that there's no sense in going on. Consider for a few moments your own background. Many parents of young children today grew up in the late 1950s, the 1960s, and the early 1970s. This was a period of advocacy for social and political change, much of it prodded by civil rights activity. There was an effort to break down barriers and have a greater acceptance of alternate lifestyles.

Still, in many families there continued to be a less-than-enlightened view of other races. More so than today, parents of a generation ago lived in neighborhoods containing people of the same racial or ethnic group. As children, many of us never had the opportunity to enter the homes of Latino, Asian, black, or white families, and there was an assumption that those environments were strange.

Even if not used in anger—and sometimes they were used with condescending goodwill—epithets like "nigger," "spic," "honky," and "chink" were part of casual conversation. We were advised, "Look after your own kind," the implication being that if you did not, there were others poised to take what you had or wanted.

There were few positive cultural influences. On TV and in the movies (with the exception of the futuristic multicultural crew of "Star Trek" and the films starring Sidney Poitier), people of color were either bad guys or objects of silly fun or caricatures like Charlie Chan. In comics, the heroes wore bright colors or white and battled black-clothed villains; in fairy tales and books, the evil witch or giant wore dark clothing; any accent was sinister; and in music the songs of nonwhite performers were associated with loose living and substance abuse.

Even games offered negative views. In 1957, the Knickerbocker Company produced a doll called the Ubangi Warrior Pop-Up, an African spear carrier whose head flew off when struck by a projectile, and around the same time board-game makers issued Chutzpah and Adventures of Little Black Sambo.

We're all products of our environment. A generation ago, that environment was fraught with stereotypes that invited us to fear or make fun of people different from ourselves.

Suppose you also think, as part of your self-examination, that—even though mentally you reject bias—there have been times when you have sent a biased message to your children. Perhaps you spent a weekend with your sister and her family who live in the next county or state. On the way home you have to drive through a racially mixed neighborhood. As you're about to enter this neighborhood you instruct your family to lock the car doors. You don't say anything else, and once you've left the neighborhood you noncommitally mention that it's okay to unlock the doors and lower the windows. This bothers you, though. You realize that as you were driving through the neighborhood your children were gazing out the window, observing people of a different color, and they might have associated locking the doors with being safe from those people. Yes, you've sent a message. Unless your children are infants, they made the connection.

We want to strongly emphasize that becoming mired in guilt during your self-examination doesn't do any good. Guilt rarely produces constructive change. And history has shown us that most people who tried to change things for the better were not saints.

To start your journey we have prepared an exercise that we hope will help you evaluate your attitudes toward other races and cultures. This is not a test, and there are no clearly right or wrong answers. But we have put the exercise in a specific context.

We began this book by noting the importance of talking to your children about race and insisting that the development of attitudes cannot be left to chance. Perhaps you've already done this, or perhaps reading this book indicates you're contemplating giving it a try.

We would like you now to consider from past experiences, or project, how you will likely feel during such a conversation. The important thing is to be honest with yourself, acknowledge how you feel, and then think about the insights we offer. Remember, the goal is for *you* to be a more open and informed parent (teacher, caregiver, community leader) on racial issues, so that *your child* will not feel uncomfortable.

Do your best to complete this statement as honestly as possible:

"When I talk to my child about race I feel . . ."

Now let's look at some possible responses:

NERVOUS.   Talking about race relations, like talking about sex, creates anxiety. It's okay to let your children know you are nervous about the subject, one reason being that they will likely sense it anyway. Yet it's important to find ways to reduce your anxiety so that you can concentrate on the discussion.

Usually, the tactics we use to curb nervousness about discussing any sensitive subject can be just as effective when race is the topic. One specific task you can do is a "dress rehearsal"—going over the issue with someone else, a sibling or a close friend, or with yourself in front of a mirror. Practice talking about race until you feel reasonably calm, and no doubt you'll find your words seem more direct and unfettered by awkward feelings. Keep in mind that you need to adapt your discussion to an age-appropriate level.

FRUSTRATED. Do you feel powerless to help your children deal with racism? Frustration occurs when you think nothing will change, no matter what you do. It may not be easy, but we assure you there is plenty you can do. In our practice we often see parents turn around troubled relationships with their children when they discover they can do things differently. Don't give up, because in most cases your child wants to discuss this topic. Free-flowing communication is vital in establishing an atmosphere where your child will feel welcome and encouraged to talk with you.

IRRITATED. You might understand your child's feelings about race, but you're also irritated because you aren't sure how to deal with them. It helps to explain to your child that you alone might not be able to solve the problem. Even if irritation is unavoidable, you must put it aside. Children will often refrain from asking questions if they sense that continuing a conversation will make you angry. It's okay to say that you are upset if something has happened that irritates you, but explore other reactions and pursue one you feel reasonably comfortable with. Once that hurdle is overcome, you'll feel more confident about continuing the conversation, and so will your child.

DISAPPOINTED. You might have made sincere and consistent efforts to promote racial tolerance . . . and then your child comes home from school and utters a racial remark. "What did I do wrong?" Disappointment can be expressed, but that should be the beginning, not the end, of the discussion. Remember, outside the home your child is being confronted with a wide array of attitudes and influences. And the remark could be an attempt to provoke a reaction so as to test the depth of your antibias views. Explain why you are disappointed, then use this opportunity to discuss the biases of others and why they are expressed by your child's peers or other adults. You can help your child understand how harmful and damaging prejudice and biased behaviors can be.

EMBARRASSED. Suppose that in a public setting like a supermarket or a social gathering your child made a negative racial remark about another person. You might not only feel embarrassed at the time but also feel guilty that before this incident you didn't bring up the subject of racial differences. Feeling embarrassed can make a conversation more awkward than it has to be. And the silver lining is that at least you've been presented with an opportunity—better late than never!

Explain how insults hurt and that they are based on inaccurate impressions. Admit that the remark could have been avoided if you had been more aware earlier of your child's curiosity or anxiety about other people. Encourage your child to go ahead and ask as many questions as he or she wants. We can all point to situations where embarrassment motivated us to set things right.

GUILTY. It simply isn't possible to protect your children from racism, so don't feel guilty when you see them troubled by something somebody said or did. You alone are not responsible for bigotry. If you were not especially aware before, you are more involved now. Guilt saps creative energy you can use to improve things. If you're hindered by guilt during a discussion, your child will think that she too is somehow at fault, and she will be reluctant to share information that could further incriminate her.

CONCERNED. Unless you come on too strong, concern is a good part of a discussion. It shows you care about racial issues and that you sincerely believe people are better off when they respect one another. Treating a discussion lightheartedly implies the topic is trivial and not worth exploring, now or in the future.

Let your child know racism is a serious issue that you are open to discussing at any time. This will impress him, and it is more likely that what he learned from a serious discussion will stay with him for a long time.

HAPPY. This might seem odd: Can you actually be happy when discussing racism? Well, we don't suggest being giddy about it, but let your child know that you're pleased she is asking questions and that it's natural to be curious about different people.

Your child should be made to feel good about what she's observing and about her courage in raising sensitive issues. Even if you don't have all the answers, she will want to approach you again with questions. Instead of being a divisive experience, discussing race is an opportunity to bring you closer together as hand in hand you explore answers.

There are myriad other emotions you might feel when considering the prospect of talking to your child about racial issues in general and, more specifically, prejudice. Don't suppress them! If you haven't looked in the mirror, objectively viewed how you feel, and then arrived at a truce with those feelings, you will not serve your child's best interests when a discussion takes place. Or worse, such a discussion will never take place, and you and your child will suffer in silence, unable to resolve feelings that will only intensify over time.

We know we're asking you to undertake what can be a big project. It's not uncommon to hear demeaning slurs on the street or in another's home, to observe people being shunned or even attacked. As children some of us were told not to associate with certain groups, and still in popular entertainment the bad guys are often those with different skin colors and accents. Prejudice is something we observe or experience in every community on a regular basis.

But that doesn't justify throwing our hands up and allowing matters to take their course. If anything, *you* are in the best position to create change for the better. It won't and it doesn't necessarily have to happen overnight. It's the little things that count.

Day after day, you are with children—as parent, teacher, caregiver. The impressions one receives in childhood influence the rest of life. Previous generations either didn't adequately address racial attitudes or imparted negative ones. Over two decades ago the U.S. Joint Commission on the Mental Health of Children recognized racism as "the number one mental health problem among America's youngsters."

Today, you can change that. Because children are now under your wing, you have a wonderful, once-in-a-lifetime opportunity to prepare children to reject prejudice. You don't have to be perfect, you just have to care and try the best you can to put into practice your good intentions.

You are not alone. In a poll conducted for *Newsweek* magazine in 1991, 72 percent of blacks and 52 percent of whites (other groups were not included in the survey) said that they would prefer to live in a neighborhood that was racially mixed, a substantial increase over a similar poll conducted three years earlier.

You can help children learn to be open and accepting of those different from themselves, to appreciate and enjoy other cultures, to challenge the bias of peers, and to thrive in a changing society. You *can* make a difference, starting right now.

3

Earlier Than You Think

It's a Saturday morning at the supermarket. Janet and Dave Ross, with their three-year-old son, Ben, are taking care of the week's food shopping. Having both parents on hand helps the shopping go twice as fast, before Ben gets too restless. He's content with a box of Animal Crackers, and all seems well for now.

Then the Rosses are startled when Ben shouts, "There's a chocolate man! Look there!" They turn to see a black man a few feet away.

Dave hurriedly says, "No, Ben, don't say that." The little boy looks at him in confusion, thinking, "What's wrong with other colors on people?"

The man looks at them, and the Rosses are very embarrassed. They are about to apologize when the man smiles. Raising his arm, he says to Ben, "It's skin, just like yours, but I'm African American and my skin is a different color."

Ben regards the man, mulling over what he's been told. Then he too smiles and holds up his arm. "I have skin. But it doesn't have any hair on it like Daddy's," he says.

"It will someday," the man remarks, then with a wave he continues his shopping.

During the next few minutes, as they finish shopping, Janet and Dave Ross explain to their son that many people in America and around the world have different-colored skin. African Americans can have brownish or black-colored skin, and so can people whose families came from India or Puerto Rico. People from China or Korea have yellow-colored skin. Native Americans have reddish skin. And they emphasize that whatever the color of their skin, people can be friends.

They know that is about all the attention Ben is willing to give the matter, and he is probably still a bit confused. At least, Janet and Dave think, their son knows that it's okay to point out color differences and to ask questions. They also decide to buy some picture books about people with different skin colors.

If your child is older than Ben, it also helps to point out that there are differences within races. Not all Latinos come from Mexico or Puerto Rico, the same way that not all whites hail from England or Germany. People from the Caribbean don't necessarily identify themselves with African Americans. The ancestry of an Asian can be traced back to Japan or Vietnam or Burma. It's important not to make quick assumptions about people based solely on skin color or accent.

For example, when eleven-year-old Consuella visited her new friend Amy, Amy's parents assumed that she was Puerto Rican. When discussing their upcoming vacation to that island, they asked Consuella to comment, but Consuella is from Cuba and knew very little about Puerto Rico. She was embarrassed and frustrated by their questions; Amy's parents thought she was being shy.

Another example: Roy's teacher did the same thing by assuming Roy is from Jamaica when in fact he is from Trinidad. It's important that we spend time getting to know individuals and not assume that they are of a certain background on the basis of our own perceptions and experiences.

Back to the supermarket: At one of the checkout counters, Bill Raymond hopes he can unload his groceries, have them totaled, and pay for them before his five-year-old daughter, Samantha, insists on having a troll doll she is admiring. Now the people in front of him, a woman and her teenage daughter, seem to be taking forever.

Suddenly Samantha points at the teenage girl and with a scowl on her face says, "She has funny-looking eyes."

Bill tries to distract his daughter and prays the Asian teenager didn't hear. But Samantha says, louder and almost accusingly, "Why does she have those funny eyes?"

Feeling helpless, Bill looks up. But the woman and her daughter have finished and are walking away. Bill hopes they aren't angry. After all, Samantha's only a little kid.

· · ·

The above incidents at the supermarket might seem basically identical, yet there is one significant difference. In both situations the child pointed to a racial characteristic that was surprising. Ben saw a person with black skin and thought of chocolate. Samantha noticed the slanted eyes of an Asian teenager. Both were naturally curious. But Samantha used the word "funny-looking" in combination with a certain facial expression. Though this isn't by any stretch of the imagination a sign of prejudice, the use of that phrase indicates that she already considers slanted eyes to be strange.

If Bill Raymond doesn't use this opportunity to discuss racial differences with his daughter, it is quite possible that this judgment, even in a five-year-old, will be the first step down the road to misunderstanding and eventually fearing people with physical characteristics different from her own.

As we mentioned in the first chapter, studies have shown that children become aware of racial differences as early as age three. This is true of children of any race. There is nothing wrong with noticing and remarking on these differences. It is all part of their incessant exploration of the huge and mysterious world around them. For very young children, every day is filled with sights, sounds, odors, and textures they experience for the first time.

It is also a natural part of development that young children begin to form generalizations, to categorize. They can separate people by gender. To a certain degree, they can group people by how large they are, by whether their voices are very high or deep, even by scent. Something that flies is a bird, something that crawls is a bug—children are dividing the ingredients of their world into general categories they can identify.

Categorizing is necessary for children, and there is nothing wrong with it in principle. In fact, categorizing helps them avoid or at least be aware of danger. If the dog next door barks furiously and is always charging into the street, children learn it falls in the "bad dog" category and are wary of going near other dogs until they are satisfied a dog is gentle. As adults, we live our lives based on information we have categorized. Of course, there are exceptions to every category, but we play the percentages.

As children notice differences in skin color and features, they categorize people according to these differences. They notice a person is black or white, brown or red or yellow, and they notice that some eyes are shaped differently from their parents' eyes. A child should never be admonished for noticing and pointing out differences. They comprise only one aspect of the wealth of information their minds are collecting and processing.

The tricky part comes when children begin to form judgments about categories. If they encounter only barking, threatening dogs, they will judge that all dogs are bad. If they are told that all bees sting and that it hurts, they could well judge that all bugs are harmful and be frightened even when an ant crawls near them.

The same is true with racial categorization. Noticing that someone has white or brown skin is just a piece of information; it doesn't indicate what kind of person he or she is or, by extension, what all white or brown people are like. If the world's worst bigot has a child, that child is not born naturally hating other groups of people. Forming a prejudice involves a learning process that uses overgeneralizations, false assumptions, stereotypes, and fear.

Obviously, one of the most effective ways to have a child view a category negatively is for the parent to express bias against that category. If you say, "White people don't like us; be careful of them," your child will become fearful of people with white skin.

Even targeting one member of a category can have the same consequence. "That Jack, the black guy, I don't trust him as far as I can throw him," you say about a co-worker who you believe is after the promotion you desire. Hearing this, your child can begin a train of thought: "Mommy doesn't like Jack. Jack is black. Black people aren't nice to Mommy. Black people aren't nice. I don't like black people." A child's mind might not contain these actual words, but to some extent he or she is beginning to form a judgment.

We don't want to make you feel cornered, believing that anything you say can and will be used against you. (We'll get into that in the next chapter!) Yet we do want to point out that your young child's view of the world expands at a rapid rate, and he or she is taking in and processing information at a level that would burst the brains of most adults. That information is being put into categories. We all need categories or there would never be any order in our lives.

Children are forming judgments about those categories earlier than you think. Samantha Raymond has formed a judgment that slanted eyes are "funny-looking." She can't be blamed for this. And the Raymonds shouldn't blame themselves. That is a waste of time. Instead, the girl's remark presents an opportunity to discuss racial differences. Continued curiosity can result in Samantha's happily noticing and then appreciating the wonder of other people's characteristics.

Let's suppose that during your child's first years you positively nurtured her awareness of racial differences. You don't think you have prejudices, or if you think you do (the fact is, we *all* have some), you have carefully refrained from expressing them. You are certain, now that your child is four or five or seven, that while she is well aware of racial differences, she has not formed any negative judgments.

For a moment, put yourself in this parent's shoes:

Grace Morgan is looking forward to being one of the mothers accompanying her daughter's Brownie troop on its annual campout. The main reason why she is excited is that her daughter, Holly, is seven, and this will be her very first camping experience.

The troop arrives at the campsite, and the Brownies begin to put up tents and collect wood for a fire. They also anxiously await a troop from another part of town that is to share the campout with them. Soon the other troop arrives, twelve young girls, half of whom are black.

Grace is happy that this has turned into an interracial campout. She and her husband believe that people of all backgrounds should be treated with respect, and though they had taught this to Holly, here was an opportunity to practice what they had preached. She pitches in with the troop leaders and the other girls, who are excited about gathering enough wood for the biggest bonfire ever.

Supper is a big success, and afterward the group of over two dozen girls and troop leaders sits in a circle around the fire roasting marshmallows on sticks. Grace becomes concerned, though, that Holly is quiet and appears barely interested in participating. Her concern turns to shock when Holly mutters, "Those black girls are hogging all the marshmallows. How come *they* always want everything!"

Grace can't believe what she heard. She wants to discuss the remark but, with all the girls there, she is afraid Holly would repeat what she'd said and cause an incident. Grace orders her daughter to her tent, and vows to deal with this totally unexpected problem in the morning.

You can bet that during that night Grace had one of those where-did-we-go-wrong discussions with herself as she tossed and turned in the tent. She and her husband had not necessarily done anything wrong. They really had done their best to raise Holly without racial bias.

But what she didn't realize is that earlier that day both troops had engaged in several running events. Both black and white girls had done well, but Holly hadn't. Holly was a reasonably good athlete, yet two months earlier she'd had a minor operation on her left knee and she still favored that leg, so much so that Holly wasn't capable of running as well as other girls her age. Now she thought of herself as a poor athlete and believed she would end up last in any contest.

Holly was angry at her circumstances. If she had performed poorly only in front of the girls in her troop, whom she'd known since kindergarten, it probably wouldn't have bothered her too much. But she believed she had embarrassed herself in front of strangers. Her self-esteem was at low ebb. And she had released some of those feelings of inadequacy by targeting the girls who were most different from herself.

There are several reasons why children raised in even the most open-minded way will express prejudice, but the primary reason is a poor self-image and a lack of self-esteem. This can be a temporary situation, as in Holly's case, or it can be a persistent problem, with a youngster believing that no matter what he or she does, just about anyone else can do it better, and that isn't fair.

Self-image describes how we imagine ourselves to be. It begins to develop when an infant first becomes aware of his or her own body and continues to be refined as the baby starts to recognize body parts. The game in which Mommy says to the baby, "Where are Tommy's eyes?"—and responds with a reassuring "Right!" when the child points to his own eyes—helps the baby practice building a self-image. As their world expands, children compare themselves to other children. Our praise, and praise from peers, moves the child along the road to a positive self-image.

Self-esteem is the feeling children have about their self-image. If children feel good about themselves, they have high self-esteem. Again, as we praise children and acknowledge their accomplishments and good behavior, their self-esteem remains at a healthy level. In a perfect world, children grow up feeling confident about their bodies and their abilities and become self-assured adults.

Alas, as we all know, it's not a perfect world, and it's the rare person whose self-esteem is never battered by outside forces. Even as adults we worry that someone can do our job better than we can, that someone is smarter or more attractive or more physically adept, or that other couples are better parents. On a daily basis, our image of ourselves and our self-confidence are constantly called into question. A very common defense mechanism is projection, which is blaming others for causing our own negative feelings.

These self-doubts are especially distressing in children. They compare themselves to peers and, after the toddler stage, even to grown-ups. Hasn't there been a time when your son or daughter has said, "I can't do that as easily as you can"? Children have simply not had enough experiences in which they have exceeded their own expectations and, perhaps, our own loftier ones. They don't have enough of a track record of successes to solidly shore up their confidence.

Part of parenting is praise. Sounds simple, doesn't it? And we all do it, to varying degrees. If our child walks, talks, draws, sings, or does anything else in a way that pleases us (and sometimes even if it doesn't!) we shower them with praise and encourage continued attempts at progress. We might feel an inner twinge of wistfulness at signs of our children growing up and attaining new levels of competence, yet the top priority is to foster a positive self-esteem that spurs them to always try to achieve and to be happy with their achievements.

Unfortunately, some parents do not give enough attention to their child's self-esteem, or as they grow older, their self-esteem is influenced by forces beyond our control. Once children are in school, a good portion of their image of themselves is affected by peers and teachers. Our role is still vitally important, but in a sense we have cast our bread upon the waters of life. A poor grade on a test, not finishing first in any sort of competition, being told certain outfits aren't "cool" or "fresh," unflattering remarks about physical attractiveness—these and other factors cause children to question their self-image.

As an adult it can be hard to shake off implications or direct assaults on our self-esteem. For some children, the toll on their emotional well-being is much greater. And that is why they are more vulnerable to acquiring prejudice.

The fact is that if we feel bad, one easy way to escape responsibility is to blame others for our perceived misfortunes. By stepping on someone else, we raise ourselves up. Children, who have not fully developed the ability of rational thought, are especially prone to this. Other than peers they simply don't like, for a variety of reasons, the most readily available targets are those who are obviously different from themselves.

For children, no matter how sensitive and aware they are, differences in color make an impression because so much of the information they process is visual. In the case of some Latinos and Asians, language or accents compound the differences. When there are problems with self-esteem, children will project these feelings on others: "It's *their* fault I couldn't do this or that" or "They're making things difficult for me." Over time these problems, if there is insufficient positive intervention, are projected on entire categories of society.

We offer one example of how, if their own problems are not properly addressed, young people can become the most volatile bias group: New Jersey reported that, in 1991, bias offenses were up 18 percent from the previous year, and the vast majority of perpetrators were between the ages of *seven and eighteen*. (In that state in 1991, racial bias accounted for 53 percent of the crimes committed!) According to Paul Goldenberg, who heads the state's bias-crime unit, the high rate of incidents among youths was caused by "a lack of self-esteem and identity. There is scapegoating of problems on other people, especially minorities. They vent their frustrations on other groups of people."

There need not be a direct relationship between a child's self-esteem problem and an experience with members of another racial group. Obviously, if your eight-year-old son got a C on a spelling test and the only classmates to receive A's were Latino, it is possible your son will feel resentment toward Latino children.

But suppose the children who performed better than your son on the test were of white, black, Latino, and Asian backgrounds? Your son could still target one group as scapegoats for his own feelings of inadequacy, because a racial difference is a target easy to see and grasp. There doesn't have to be a rational connection. Your son's self-esteem was jeopardized and he blamed others—the ones most visibly different.

We should point out that we're talking about chronic self-esteem problems. Doing poorly on one test doesn't necessarily mean that your son will form a bias. The more likely scenario is that the test was one indication of his struggle with spelling, a persistent problem that has eaten away at his confidence. If your child doesn't win one running event, she's disappointed but will go out there next time and try to win the contest. If, like Holly Morgan, there is an extended period during which she doesn't do well in athletic events, this period of perceived failure influences her to think she is a poor athlete and probably will always be one.

That's a harsh belief, difficult for a child's self-esteem to withstand. A common way to soften the pain is to hold others responsible—those of a different gender, class, or race—by scapegoating. The seeds of poor self-esteem can be planted early, and if their feelings are left unresolved, some children tend to grasp at the straw of scapegoating down the road.

We also want to point out that just as problems with self-esteem (along with insecurity and interpersonal anxiety) can lead to prejudice, expressions of prejudice can lead to self-esteem problems. Though white children are subjected to prejudice, in the majority of cases the victims are people of color. Many Latino, Asian, Native American, and African American children grow up in environments in which they are told or see in the media that their racial group is presented as inferior. Some children of color not only develop poor self-esteem but can gradually internalize the idea that everything would be all right if they were white.

For example, in our study involving black preschoolers' perception of white dolls and black dolls, three-quarters of the black children chose the black doll as "bad." When asked preference questions, such as if they would like to play with a black doll or a white doll, two out of three children chose the white doll. These results revealed that racism as a learning process could foster self-esteem problems in very young children. More important, they also indicated that the children were aware of society's messages concerning race and that white was projected as more desirable, or at least the acceptable norm.

You might be asking now, "How can I tell if my child is having a self-esteem problem? And how do I know that problem is leading to biased attitudes?"

Resentful children are not very discreet, and chances are that at some point you will hear your child express prejudice. The statement can be very simple, such as "I don't like black (white) people!" It can be a bit more subtle, such as "If *they* weren't at my school, I'd get to be on the safety patrol." These and similar expressions are clear indications that your youngster is scapegoating on the basis of racial differences.

But to nip the problem in the bud, it's necessary to be alert to what your child is thinking. Every child at some point has a self-esteem challenge, and many children manage to overcome the challenge without intervention. It's part of the ebb and flow of childhood. The key is to detect when the challenge has become a chronic problem.

The following are some signs of the low self-esteem that makes children vulnerable to acquiring prejudiced attitudes:

DISRESPECT. Children behave inappropriately toward parents, other family members, and possibly other adults. Sometimes children are unaccountably rude and might not mean to be so, but if there's a pattern of rudeness, your child may be feeling inferior and full of resentment.

SELF-DEFEATING BEHAVIOR. Children seem to deliberately perform simple tasks poorly or claim there's no way they can complete a school assignment. They don't feel up to doing what other youngsters their age might take for granted.

FEELINGS OF INADEQUACY. Children are unlikely to even try to do something like buckle a seat belt or add 4 + 4. "Why try? I can't do it." Every child faces a situation when he or she isn't confident about solving a problem or accomplishing something, but when he fails on a regular basis to try, he is feeling chronically inadequate.

WITHDRAWAL. Youngsters can withdraw into a fantasy world, attempting to block out the rejection they feel from other people. Involvement in fantasy is not by itself unhealthy; it's good for children to stretch their imaginations. But if your child would rather indulge in fantasy than associate with other children (for example, her dolls are her real friends) or even family members, that indicates she is unhappy with what the real world offers.

TROUBLE AT SCHOOL. We all like to believe that our children are perfect angels in the classroom. However, it's the rare child who is not devilish sometimes due to boredom or the distraction of a beautiful spring day or "So-and-so got me in trouble." It happens. But when the teacher reports that your youngster is often disruptive, acts out, is hostile or belligerent, that usually indicates a self-esteem problem.

SELF-DEPRECATING REMARKS. Does your child regularly say negative things about herself? It's okay for a child to be modest, but it's a problem when she frequently judges herself in a harsh and unfair manner, blaming herself constantly or denigrating her appearance.

BRAGGING. Every child looks for praise, and sometimes they exaggerate their accomplishments. But some children display an urgent need to be recognized as larger than life. There's nothing they can't do, and do better than anyone else. If you find yourself growing weary of having to bestow constant praise, and even then it's not enough, your child is struggling with self-esteem.

LACK OF SOCIALIZATION. Your child would rather slump on the couch than go out and play. When placed in a situation with other children, she sits off to the side or wanders away to be by herself as the others become involved in a game. Every child needs some time alone, but if too frequently she is isolated from peers, that indicates she fears how other children will treat her.

. . .

We sincerely hope you have not recognized your child in any of the above descriptions. But if you have, that doesn't mean your youngster is doomed to a life filled with psychological and emotional trauma that will include racial bigotry. Remember, the goal now is to recognize the signs. Then resolve the problem and avoid your child's becoming a dysfunctional adolescent. You are, in a sense, lucky to notice a sign of a self-esteem problem, because it means your child is calling out for help.

How can you help? Get involved . . . right now! How do you get involved in improving your child's self-esteem? Some people seek professional help for their children. Of course, as practicing psychologists we heartily endorse such help, yet in many cases that help can come from within the family. Parenting is the oldest and most important profession, and here we offer you a few suggestions.

• It might seem too obvious to urge praise, but for some parents this isn't obvious enough. Even the most well-intentioned parents may be distracted by their own problems, work pressures, or their relationship; they may overlook the fact that their children are seeking encouragement and praise for the smallest accomplishments.
• If there are indications that your child is struggling at school, look for tutorial help to improve academic achievement. Consider a tutor of a different race who is likely to offer your child a new or fresh educational perspective.
• Spend time with your child—if you have more than one, then do it individually—participating in fun and challenging activities. Visit a cultural center, take a walk or drive, share an after-school snack at the park, or select books at a library together.
• Become involved with your child in a structured group activity, such as a sport, a church group, a community event. Look for one that is multiracial.
• Sometimes you can help by providing a positive influence. One example is having an older sibling or neighbor you trust spend time with your child. If possible, arrange for a companion who is of another race.
• Help your child to develop problem-solving skills through modeling, coaching, and support. One method is to develop several situations

that risk harming self-esteem and to discuss with your child the best way to deal with each situation. In the long run, resolving dilemmas for your youngster can cause other problems. Take time now to help your children think of sensible ways to resolve their own dilemmas.

Unless they are imitating a parent's blatantly expressed attitude and thereby winning approval, children do not inherently want to be prejudiced. Any joy one feels over insulting someone of another race is temporary and usually leaves a feeling of uneasiness. The initial underlying feelings of frustration and hostility remain unresolved, only to be aimed at the next safe and available target.

Unfortunately, children with self-esteem problems often can't help themselves. When they feel low, a way to not feel any lower, and perhaps temporarily feel a bit better, is to think or declare that someone else is even lower. The most readily apparent and usually available target is the person who is the most different, and with few exceptions, it's that person with skin of another color, with an accent, or with "funny-looking" eyes.

You can prevent a prejudice problem from developing. The following anecdote provides an example:

Eliza Martino, eight years old, was having some problems in school, and the administrators decided she could be better helped in a slower track. Believing there was a stigma attached to this and jolted by what she considered a demotion, Eliza was angry and frustrated. Even at the new level, she performed poorly. She didn't discuss her feelings with her parents, fearing they would be disappointed in her.

She focused her feelings on several black classmates, kept dwelling on her feelings, and then finally one night, when she was doing her homework, Eliza declared, "Black people are stupid!"

Her parents were startled. What did this have to do with their daughter's school performance? But instead of ignoring the remark, her parents asked her about her feelings, and in the ensuing discussion they better understood all that Eliza was experiencing and saw that she was projecting her negative feelings onto others.

The Martinos took two steps. One was to request that the school provide tutoring for Eliza, so that one-on-one she was able to improve her skills. The other was that with the help of school personnel they were able to point out black students in higher tracks and gifted classes as well as in her track. This impressed upon Eliza that one's color did not determine one's academic ability.

As she did better in school and her frustration waned, her self-esteem improved. When asked about black students, Eliza announced, "They are pretty smart . . . like me!"

4

An Ounce of Prevention . . .

In the first chapter, we asked you to look in the mirror and reflect upon your own racial attitudes. Here we want to take that self-examination several steps farther, to see how your attitudes become evident to children, how communication is essential in combatting prejudice, and how parents (and other caregivers) need to be active participants in responding to bias situations.

Let's assume, as we suggested, that you took a time-out to thoroughly examine your attitudes. Some of you may have been aghast; others of you may have thought that your attitudes were reasonably balanced, with only a few you'd like to work on; and the rest of you may believe your attitudes are perfectly healthy. To the last group there is something we want to stress very strongly: *No one is without bias!*

Are we saying that we're all bigots but some of us are better at burying prejudice? Of course not. There is an enormous distance between those who are intentionally bigots and the rest of us. Bigots hate people different from themselves, associate with others only when forced to, and make a point of letting the people around them know their unwholesome views. Hatred is a pervasive presence in their minds, and in some cases, like membership in extremist organizations and acts of violence, this hatred is made very clear. Such people will *teach* their children prejudice.

Thankfully, most of us are not bigots. We do have some conscious or unconscious biased feelings that we might not understand and probably realize are unhealthy. Even if we've made sincere efforts during our lives to suppress or rid ourselves of fear, mistrust, and anger toward other races, it is the rare person who has completely eliminated them. Many of us grew up in environments in which, due to the influence of adults, the media, and other forces in society, we were made to feel uncomfortable or even suspicious of people who are different.

Do not feel bad about uncomfortable feelings. The key is to acknowledge your discomfort and to assure that your children will grow up in a more open environment and not *develop* prejudice. Widespread, positive change will not occur all at once in one generation. But you have an opportunity now to create positive changes in your children's lives and establish a solid foundation for positive changes in future generations.

"Sounds like a tall order!" you exclaim. "How can I possibly begin?" Don't feel overwhelmed. We'll begin one step at a time.

One step involves common sense. In the previous chapter, we discussed the factors that can make a child vulnerable to prejudice. Overall, the most important thing you can do as a parent is provide an open, caring, supportive environment for your youngster. As best you can, avoid injuring his self-esteem. For example, if your child is having difficulty completing a task, don't say, "You're so slow. Why can't you work faster than that?" or withdraw your attention when he does something incorrectly. Obviously, being critical will produce a wide range of problems, and it is likely prejudice will be one of them.

Okay, you are pretty confident that you are providing a good environment, that whatever your personal circumstances, you're doing the best you can. What of those uncomfortable feelings about other racial groups? However noble your intentions, the fact is you won't wake up one morning and find them gone. Accept that you have them. The next step is to prevent their being accepted by your child. Indeed, actions you take for your child's sake will very likely have a positive effect on your own attitudes, no matter how ingrained they are.

Many parents who harbor biased feelings think that they can successfully hide those feelings: You wouldn't stop a black or brown or white child from playing with your youngster; you don't utter racial epithets; and you would never ridicule people of other races whom you see on the street or on television shows. You think that by doing nothing wrong, you are doing something right.

Well, yes, that's true . . . up to a point. You are not demonstrating bias. You have suppressed your feelings. But over time those feelings will come out, and you may not be aware of what we call subtle signals.

You don't need Western Union to send a message. Young children are extremely perceptive beings. They pick up on the tiniest bits of information. This is especially true with their parents. They are always watching you; they are very sensitive to your moods; they observe your body language; they hear in your tone of voice what's really behind your words; and even by touch they can detect your emotions. They might not understand much of the information they collect, but it has an impact on their own moods, feelings, and attitudes.

On a daily basis you send out subtle signals that convey your feelings about race. Here's one example:

Rose Lundgren and her five-year-old son, Kenny, are in a department store. It's a few days before kindergarten begins, and because Kenny grew like a weed over the summer, he needs some new clothes.

The children's clothing department is on the fourth floor. There is an escalator, but because Kenny can't resist fooling around on escalators, Rose is afraid he'll get a foot caught, so hand in hand they wait for the elevator. When the doors open, Rose sees that the only occupant of the elevator is a Latino man.

She hesitates, and involuntarily her hand squeezes Kenny's. But after a moment, Rose and her son enter. The man gets off on the third floor. After the doors close, she releases Kenny's hand, immediately forgetting that they had shared the elevator with another person.

In this situation, the mother did not make any remark about the Latino man, nor did she even have any conscious negative thought. It would never occur to her that Kenny noticed anything. Yet in a very subtle way, a message was sent. The youngster sensed the hesitation, and he felt the tightened grip on his hand. His mother was nervous. Why? There was a man with brown skin in the elevator. Was he dangerous? Should I be nervous about men with brown skin?

Sometimes, children will voice these thoughts. Unfortunately, parents could be embarrassed and deny that even for a split second they felt fear, and so they may dismiss any questions. An opportunity to acknowledge feelings and discuss why they are inappropriate is then lost. And many times parents are simply unaware that their feelings were apparent and will accuse the child of imagining things.

Here are a few other examples of subtle signals:

• When you socialize in your home with friends and neighbors, are guests from other racial groups few and far between? Nonexistent?
• Upon arriving at a playground, do you automatically steer your child toward children of the same race as yours?
• Do you hesitate to allow a repairman of another race to enter your home, when a week or two earlier one of the same race as you was casually admitted?
• When you and your child get on a bus or train and there are several empty seats, do you choose seats next to a passenger of the same race?
• When you buy an action figure, a doll, or another toy for your child, does the figure or the packaging always feature the same race as yours?
• If you celebrate Christmas or Hanukkah, it might be a common practice to exchange cards with friends. Very often friends with children enclose family photos or photos just of the children. With people you rarely see, it's a way to keep in touch with one another's history. We like to attach these photos to the refrigerator with magnets. Take a look this holiday season: Do any of the photos on display for your family portray a family of another race?
• It might simply come down to asking yourself, "Do I have a black (white, Latino, Asian, Native American) friend?" Is there anyone you care about, and who cares about you, who is of a different race?

We don't expect that parents will stop sending these signals just by willpower. For one thing, our little body movements and other signs have become like habits. It's hard enough to break habits in children; in adults, responses have become deep-seated. While the signals may reflect deeply ingrained attitudes, we urge you to continue to work on changing those attitudes. In the meantime we also encourage you not to dwell on the messages sent to your children. They are going to happen. And remember, guilt is counterproductive.

What can you do? Be alert for when you've sent a subtle signal and use that occasion as an opportunity to discuss racial attitudes with your child. You might not be able to do so immediately. Some settings are obviously inappropriate, and this issue should be discussed at a time and place that's comfortable for you and your child.

There is an exercise we use in our practice that has proved helpful for adults and children in understanding their racial attitudes. We offer here part of that exercise—which we call the Hopson RAP (Racial Attitude Assessment Procedure)—and we ask you to do it with your child. (Some questions are for children only.) The answers given will provide a wealth of material for frank, open discussions and insight into your comfort level with people of other races.

Please complete the following sentences (and feel free to switch the racial group around):

1. Black people are . . .
2. White people are . . .
3. I like Asian people who . . .
4. I don't like Latino people who . . .
5. When I see black people in my neighborhood, I think . . .
6. In school, Asian people . . .
7. At the playground, white people . . .
8. My greatest fear of Latino people is . . .
9. Native American people are best at . . .
10. My parents think that Asians are . . .
11. My parents don't invite black friends because . . .
12. If I had one wish concerning race relations it would be that . . .
13. White is positive because . . .
14. What I have most in common with Latinos is . . .
15. I sometimes call blacks . . .

There is no scoring involved, no pass or fail. But by thinking carefully and giving candid answers you'll have, we think, a better idea of your feelings toward other races. Having your child do the same will indicate what attitudes he or she has already formed and their extent.

If you are disturbed by a couple of your child's answers . . . good! No, we're not sadists. We don't want you to feel bad, but the distressing answers mean your child felt comfortable enough with you to respond honestly, and you now know what areas need to be addressed. The next step is to talk to your child.

As a parent, you already know that very often an issue that requires discussion will be brought up first by your youngster. With sex, race, religion, substance abuse, or any other sensitive issue, you might have an idea about when it would be appropriate to raise the subject, then

—wham!—they ask a question that surprises or even shocks you. Your first reaction is probably, "No, wait. You're too young to know about that!"

The fact is, your child doesn't know, but the question confirms he's curious and has been for a while. No matter how startled you are, please remember that *asking* the question and asking *you* means you must have a pretty good relationship. You have his trust: He'd rather have a response from you than from anyone else, and your answer can relieve curiosity more than one received from peers, other adults, or teachers.

Of course, some children don't ask questions about an issue they are intensely curious about. Why not? One reason may be that at an earlier age, questions they asked were rebuffed or answered insincerely. More specifically, if a child has previously hinted at curiosity about race but is silent about it now, you may have overlooked or casually dismissed it.

Some children are more reserved than others. They are prone to ruminate over things that interest them and they prefer to find their own answers. And unfortunately some children have had their questions answered outside the home—by peers or an ill-informed adult or the media—before there was a good opportunity to ask their parents. The overall advantages of this can be endlessly debated, but a fact of life in the 1990s is that many children spend as much or more time at day-care centers, preschool and after-school programs, and with extended-family members or other adults, than with their parents. So questions are asked of others or not asked at all.

In this case, parents have to be especially sensitive to their child's moods and behavior. If you are, you can detect when your child is pondering or is troubled by an issue she can't (or shouldn't) resolve by herself. It is then absolutely necessary that you initiate a discussion. We hope it's easy, but many times it will take gentle prodding and encouragement. Don't give up. Don't think, "Well, if she doesn't want to talk to me, she doesn't want to talk to me." Right under your nose, attitudes are being formed and judgments are being made that a few years from now will be extremely difficult to change.

Sometimes, even in the most recalcitrant child, events will trigger a discussion. Two examples are the incidents in Los Angeles—the videotaped beating of Rodney King that was shown on TV repeatedly in the spring of 1991, and then a year later the violent protest that followed the acquittal of the four officers accused of the assault. We received numerous calls after these incidents from parents who wanted to know how to respond to the questions their children were asking.

Other times, children will ask questions after participating in or observing a racial incident at school or at a park, or they are upset by the vehemence of a racial slur. We advise parents that the worst thing they can do is gloss over or react in an emotionally intense manner to the incident and its implications. What they can do is talk to their children, encourage them to express how they feel about the incident, admit that the world contains conflict but that not all people are violent or filled with hatred toward others.

However, you can't—nor should you—wait for something to happen and then strap on your armor to combat prejudice. By definition, being a hero means that through deep concern and decisive action you've successfully overcome steep odds. The better approach can be less glamorous but in the long run more effective: Prevent the odds of forming unwholesome attitudes from increasing.

As with most child-rearing issues, it's best to be prepared. Here we offer typical questions children ask about race and suggest appropriate responses (adapt them depending on your child's age):

• *Why am I this color?* People come in several races and many colors because of where their ancestors lived. Skin color helped living in different climates. Our ancestors came from _____.

• *Why do _____ people talk funny?* People speak different languages and have different expressions and mannerisms. One is not better than the other.

• *Why do so many _____ people hate us?* We hear and see _____ people who seem to hate. Not all _____ hate other people. (Point out an example of positive race relations, such as a community project or a social action involving people of various races working together.)

• *Are _____ people better than _____ people?* No. There are many great _____ people and many great _____ people. No group is better than another.

- *Why were _____ people treated badly?* Many years ago _____ people were treated unfairly. We still have to work toward having everyone given the same rights and equal treatment.

Yes, it's a cliche that "an ounce of prevention is worth a pound of cure," but like most cliches, this one is based on fact. With racial issues, serious consideration of questions followed by open-minded discussions sets a pattern that encourages your child to come to you first and goes a long way toward preventing negative attitudes from forming. Think about what you do on a daily basis to prevent your youngster from contracting an illness or from feeling bad about himself, peers, relatives, or even you. That kind of caring is necessary to protect against developing prejudice.

Thus far we have talked about your role as parents—assessing your own attitudes and being open to questions. That is the prevention aspect. Now we want to take another step with you, and that is intervention.

Though few parents are happy about it, many have the philosophy that once a child is old enough to explore a little more of his world, his parents pretty much have to accept what happens. If your daughter has learned to ride a bike, you can't keep running out in the street to prevent her from going too fast. If your son has learned how to play basketball, you can't hover at the playground to warn him about the possibility of twisting an ankle. We wince and cringe and pray they will be all right, and just in case, we have Band-Aids and ice packs handy. Experiencing situations of moderate risk is part of a child's natural development.

We don't advocate this same live-and-let-live philosophy when it comes to prejudice. There are situations in which your child is not in physical danger but without intervention is at risk of acquiring (or reinforcing) attitudes that jeopardize his or her emotional well-being.

What are these situations? They can be subtle, but just like messages you send, they can have an impact.

Nearly every day Priscilla Kady brings her son, Henry, who is six, to the local playground after school. His favorite activities are climbing on the monkey bars and hurtling down the circular slide. Usually he tries the other attractions first, then gets down to business on his favorites. Priscilla enjoys these outings because her son is getting fresh air and exercise, while off to the side she relaxes with the other parents.

Then Priscilla noticed something, and she didn't know how long it had been happening: It appeared that Henry was avoiding the black children at the playground. He would interrupt his round of activities by skipping one where a black youngster was playing. And if any black children were on the monkey bars or the circular slide, he wouldn't go there at all.

At first Priscilla thought she was imagining things. Then after several afternoons she became convinced that Henry was purposely avoiding black children. "Well, what's the big deal?" she thought. "It's just a phase he's going through. He'll get over it." Priscilla resolved to wait it out.

But she couldn't shake the feeling that something was going on inside her son, something that upset or even scared him. And looking around her, Priscilla noticed that all the parents she stood with were white, while groups of black and Latino parents gathered separately at another side of the playground. It wasn't so much that she had accepted this division of races—she just hadn't been aware of it before.

One afternoon, after leaving the park, Priscilla stopped off at an ice-cream shop. Henry was thrilled; his mom always said treats would spoil his dinner! Priscilla used this opportunity to ask her son why he avoided the black children. She began by inquiring if this was something he was aware of.

The little boy nodded. After more gentle questions, Henry revealed that in school a group of black first-graders had teased him in gym class because he couldn't do chin-ups. Some of them couldn't do chin-ups either, yet Henry felt they were ganging up and making fun of him. So, at the playground, he didn't want to do anything where black kids could see him. They were bad kids, he said, because they unfairly thought they were better than he was.

For a moment Priscilla thought about making a joke, telling Henry to let it slide, that he would eventually get over the discomfort. But it bothered her that he had labeled the black children bad. She asked her son if he had ever been teased about anything else. Henry said he had and offered a couple of instances. After reassuring him that all children get teased at one time or another, and that as a youngster she had experienced her share, Priscilla asked why this time he had focused on black classmates. Henry replied that he thought there was probably something wrong with people who have dark skin—or else why does his mother always stay away from them at the playground?

Inwardly, Priscilla sighed. She realized she hadn't avoided the other parents on purpose. That's just the way things were at the park—and, it occurred to her, elsewhere too.

As they finished their ice creams, she told her son that he shouldn't separate his classmates by the color of their skin and that adults shouldn't do the same with other adults. She made a bargain with Henry: If he would go ahead and use all of the playground equipment, she would help him do chin-ups at home and she would try to be friendly with all the parents. After a week, they would compare their feelings. Her son agreed, and they shook sticky hands.

For a few days Henry was still tentative about using some of the playground equipment, and during that time Priscilla observed that he kept looking at her. For a few minutes each day she talked with either the black or Latino parents, to herself noting that the conversations were identical—how their children were doing at school, their jobs, the local government, views of national events. She did feel uncomfortable at first, but then realized that as parents they had similar concerns and situations to laugh about.

At the end of the week, mother and son went out for ice cream again. (Secretly, Henry thought, "I'll be glad to talk to Mom about any problems if we get to do this," while Priscilla thought, "I hope we don't have to talk about too many problems, or I'll have to go on a diet!") Henry said the other kids were cool and that one of them had shown him how to go down the slide backwards on his stomach. Another had told him about visiting his grandmother in Puerto Rico, where it's actually summer all the time.

Priscilla reported that all the parents loved their children and wanted them to grow up strong and healthy. As Henry licked his last bit of ice cream, he said, "I'm glad I put you guys together. Now us kids can be friends, too!"

Sometimes we think, "Oh, if life could only be like that." We have news for you: It can. Not every situation can be happily resolved, and most situations require time and consistent effort. Whenever you have doubts, please keep in mind that you can make a difference in your child's life.

Being ready, willing, and able to respond to situations is the best way to achieve rewarding results. Here are some typical scenarios and examples of how you can intervene:

• Your seven-year-old daughter returns home from having dinner at a classmate's home. Her friend is Latino. Your daughter reports that the food tasted funny and that they must eat strange stuff all the time.

You can explain that just because certain foods are different from the kind your family usually eats, that doesn't mean anything is wrong with it. There are many foods that different peoples brought to this country and that your family routinely eats—such as pizza, egg rolls, enchiladas, and pita bread. With your daughter, you can research what foods familiar to us today came from other parts of the world, and perhaps once a week you can try foods associated with other racial and ethnic groups.

• It's your son's eighth birthday, and invited to the party are friends on his block and a few classmates. During the festivities, a neighbor's youngster, referring to two white boys, says loud enough for all to hear: "What are those guys doing here?" You can see your son is upset, and the two boys are clearly uncomfortable.

Poor intervention would be to announce "It's time for cake!" as a way to distract the youngsters. This implies the remark is acceptable or insignificant.

The most desirable response is for your son to take the initiative in telling his neighbor how he feels about the remark (sad, angry, surprised) and in explaining that those two classmates are at the party because they, too, are friends. However, your son might be reluctant to risk a confrontation with a longtime playmate. You, then, can offer the same response and emphasize that all of your son's friends are welcome in your home. It would also be a good idea to discuss your son's feelings with him after the others have left.

• Your family is having lunch on Sunday after having attended church. Your nine-year-old daughter mentions that a girl she knows goes to a different church and that recently a classmate confided, "I don't know why those people go to church, because God isn't black."

None of us can say with any certainty what color God is—or if God is any color at all! (And there is much debate among historians over the skin color of Jesus Christ.) This should be discussed with your daughter. Many people of all colors go to churches, synagogues, and mosques to worship God. What's more important is your religious beliefs and love for all humankind.

• After picking up your five-year-old son from school, you notice he appears angry. When you inquire, he says, "I wanted to be on the spelling team, but the teacher said Juan could be on it. You know what? He's a spic!"

Some parents might exclaim, "Don't say things like that!" In young children, racial epithets can have the same distressing force as a four-letter word, and we react with shock and anger. But the issue here is your son's anger. Why was he so upset at not being selected for the team?

It could turn out that he's been having some trouble with spelling, and being left off the team was like pouring salt on a wound to his self-esteem. He focused his anger on a youngster of a different race, the most apparent target. You should (1) discuss any spelling difficulties and promise to work with him to resolve them, (2) say firmly that you disapprove of such racial terms because they hurt people, and (3) have a talk with your son's teacher to find out if there is an emerging problem with the youngster's using racial slurs. This will help you determine if further intervention is needed on the teacher's part as well.

• Your eight-year-old daughter and a few friends are playing in the backyard. Suddenly, you overhear one girl announce, "She's sneaky, like all chinks are!"

Again a racial slur, yet the problem is compounded because an unattractive and inaccurate judgment about an entire group of people is being promoted. You could go outside and say, "I'm concerned about what you just said. What made you say it?"

True, the child might feel intimidated and your daughter could feel uncomfortable, but intervention is necessary. Encourage all the youngsters to discuss their feelings about Asians, and perhaps other groups, and be a good listener—you're not a prosecutor. To foster empathy you could gently add, "How would you feel if someone was saying something bad about you?" Hopefully, the children will be given a new perspective on racial prejudice, but at the very least your daughter has been sent a clear message that such bias is unacceptable.

• Out of the blue, your six-year-old daughter says, "You know, with the skin brown people have, they look dirty. What's the matter with them? Don't they take baths?"

This raises an issue common to all children, the standard of beauty. In the media, and especially the advertising industry, white is most often associated with attractiveness and good health. And it's not rare for very young children to think that black or brown can be washed off to reveal clean (white) skin. You should explain that beauty has nothing to do with color, nor does cleanliness. To further display and model an appreciation of the diversity of people, it would be helpful to buy a doll with a different skin color and emphasize how pretty it is.

• Your eight-year-old son, who loves baseball, seems increasingly reluctant to go to the Little League games his team plays. Finally, he announces he's not going anymore. When you ask why, he says, "The black kids are always acting wild and they scare me. Why can't they just act like normal people?"

You could just allow your son to stay home, hoping he'll get over his fear. It is more likely, though, that over time fear of black peers will become ingrained and he will be unhappy playing any sport.

It might be true that some black youngsters are more expressive on the field. But this is not directed at your son, and they certainly don't want to hurt him. You should explain that it's healthy for people to express their feelings openly and in a variety of ways. Certainly one way is to cheer loudly or jump up and down. All different kinds of behavior qualify as being normal.

Explore other aspects of your son's experience at Little League. Perhaps he has been having trouble hitting or catching the ball. You could take time to practice with him or, even better, at the next game see if one or two of the black children could stay later or come over to your home for extra practice.

• Your five-year-old daughter says she likes everybody in her kindergarten class, even the girl who is different. When you ask why she's different, your daughter replies, "Because she has a black (brown, white, yellow) face."

It's normal for your child to be aware that one or more classmates has skin color different from her own. And just by saying the color is different she hasn't necessarily expressed bias or even discomfort. Yet this is an excellent opportunity to discuss with your youngster the cultural background of her classmate and the traits that she has in common with this child. By doing this, you are teaching an appreciation of differences and an understanding that people shouldn't be stereotyped by skin color.

• We'd like to add one way that your intervention wouldn't be helpful, and that's the use of positive stereotyping. With good intentions, you might look for ways to compliment people of other races. Examples are "Asians are smart," "African Americans are good athletes," "White people speak well," or "Latinos are great cooks."

Your motivation could be to say something nice about another racial group so that your child will appreciate at least one characteristic. But in a subtle way you are categorizing people by race, and by emphasizing one good quality (which may or may not be true), you imply that in other areas they don't do so well.

Suppose you're watching a basketball game with your son or daughter and Michael Jordan or Chris Webber or Patrick Ewing soars for a monster jam. Thrilled, you exclaim, "Those people are marvelous athletes!" You think that all you've done is express admiration. But in a sense you're limiting your youngster's perspective: "Those people" —and people of any color—are also marvelous scientists, politicians, physicians, and business leaders.

A book could be written just on the situations you and your child might face daily that involve fear, mistrust, or a lack of understanding of other racial and ethnic groups. Even though we have offered only a small sample, we hope you see how our recommended courses of action stress that intervention is necessary.

Don't ever believe "he didn't understand what was said" or "she'll get over it." Being passive means a problem will only fester. A child left without your guidance will form his or her own conclusions, almost always negative ones. Without intervention he or she might also suffer in silence, and in this way may learn to bury feelings instead of talking with you.

In this chapter we've talked about your subtle signals, the need for open communication between you and your youngster, and corrective action. Let's suppose you are ready to work hard in your home on racial problems, and you are creating an atmosphere conducive to open, candid discussions. But wait—you don't hold all the cards! Though you are the most important influence in your child's life, there are others.

In the next chapter we'll look at what happens when people your child considers authority figures—relatives, neighbors, friends— enter your home, or your child enters theirs, and you see your well-intentioned plans go out the window.

5
Relatively Speaking

It's a Saturday afternoon, and Sally Renfield has a classmate over to her house. This is the first time Sally has spent time with Denise outside of school, yet right away they start a board game, then paint pictures, then play on the backyard swing set, and before they know it, three hours have passed.

Sally's mother, Beth, is pleased that the six-year-olds get along so well together. Because the Renfields live in a predominantly white neighborhood, there are few opportunities for Sally to associate with children of other races. As Sally was developing a friendship with Denise, the girl had expressed curiosity about black skin and about the "different" children in general whom she encountered at school. The Renfields had answered her questions as best they could and had read her stories that featured youngsters of all races. When her daughter said that "Denise is a lot of fun," Beth had encouraged setting up a play date.

When a car pulls up outside, Beth assumes it is Denise's father come to pick up his daughter. Instead, Beth's mother enters, arriving early for dinner. "Hi, Nana!" Sally calls, as she and Denise skip into the living room. "Watch what we can do!"

The girls do somersaults, somehow managing to avoid the furniture, and then finish with a curtsy and gales of laughter. A horn sounds, and peering out the window, Denise announces her father is here. Sally tells her friend good-bye after promising that she would play at Denise's home the following weekend.

"She seemed like a nice girl," Nana says, settling herself on the couch and inviting Sally to sit beside her. "Looked like you two were having fun together."

"Oh, yes!" Sally exclaims. "She likes to play the same things I do."

"That's good." Nana looks at Beth. "It's a shame, isn't it, that those people can have such nice children, but then they grow older and get into trouble."

"What trouble, Nana?" Sally asks, with obvious concern.

"Oh, never mind. Here, look at the dessert I brought."

Beth is stunned by her mother's remark. It is inappropriate and certainly inaccurate, but she decides not to say anything and risk further remarks. Sally is distracted by the box of cupcakes. She's already forgotten it, Beth thinks. Why raise a red flag?

Many of us have relatives who have views different from our own, especially if they are a generation older. And many of us have learned that one way to maintain harmony within families is to avoid discussions on politics, religion, and race. "Why get into a needless dispute?" we say to ourselves. "They will believe what they want to believe; I can't change that. Everybody's entitled to an opinion, and I can raise my children the way I want."

It's true that one of the fundamental principles of our democracy is that individuals have the right to hold and express their opinions, even if we are vehemently opposed to them. A comment attributed to Voltaire is "I disapprove of what you say, but I will defend to the death your right to say it." Expressions of prejudice, as distasteful and wrong as they are, fall into this category.

Yet that does not mean we must accept the effect biased remarks have on our children. How powerful is that effect? After their parents, young children are highly influenced by and model the behavior of the other adults they have frequent contact with—and the more intimate the relationship, the more profound the influence. A close relationship between a child and an extended-family member can be a double-edged sword: On the one hand, Nana or Uncle Jack can provide fun and comfort, yet on the other hand, if they hold attitudes we don't approve of, our youngster's impressionable mind is influenced in ways we can't control.

This is especially true of grandparents. Our mothers and fathers grew up during a time when there were fewer bridges between racial groups. Some attitudes considered objectionable today were accepted as normal or at least sensible decades ago. We're not calling your parents bigots. We're simply pointing out that, whatever their color, they are the products of a society that mistrusted or feared racial and ethnic differences.

Most of us are pleased if our children have a close relationship with grandparents, aunts, and uncles. Our society has become very mobile, with people rarely staying and raising their families in the neighborhoods they grew up in. One disadvantage of this is that children are not raised surrounded by an extended family unit, people who love and care for our children almost as much as we do. When there is frequent and loving contact between generations, the emotional health of growing children is enhanced.

But if that contact also involves prejudice, children are presented with attitudes we cannot ignore. However enlightened our approach, there is an adverse impact. It's as if we're trying to build something, and for every two bricks we place, someone takes away one.

After family members, other adults have an influence. Typically these people are neighbors and friends, people who send their children to the same schools and day-care centers, and whom we socialize with. We may not grant these people any particular authority over our children, as we might with family members, yet just the fact that they are adults with whom we have an emotional relationship means our children look up to them and are usually comfortable with what they say and how they act.

One other category of influence in our homes is an older sibling. Some parents have youngsters with substantial age gaps—especially with the high rate of divorce and the increasing number of stepfamilies and blended families. In long-term marriages, couples are choosing to have children well into their thirties, after having had a child in their twenties. An older sibling can bring home attitudes and behaviors that create difficulty for a young sister or brother.

Roger Marsh and his five-year-old son, Kenny, drive into town to Roger's favorite barber shop. After parking the car, they walk down the street hand in hand. Suddenly, Roger feels his son draw back.

"What's wrong?" Roger asks.

Kenny doesn't answer, but there is an expression of fear on his face. Following his son's gaze, Roger sees a policeman approaching from the opposite direction. The policeman waves hello as he passes. Once he is some distance away, Roger feels his son's grip relax.

"Why were you scared?" Roger asks, kneeling to his son's level.

"He's a bad policeman," Kenny mutters.

"Why do you think so?"

"He's white. All white policeman are bad."

"Who told you that?"

"Steven did."

With gentle prodding, the story comes out. Steven, fourteen, is Roger's other son. Apparently some incidents reported in the news had convinced Steven that white cops routinely hate and harm black people, particularly teenagers. Even though Steven had not had direct experience with this, he had warned his younger brother, "Just wait until you get older. Then it'll be your turn. You better watch out."

Roger realizes that he and his wife have their work cut out for them. They both work at corporations with very strong equal-opportunity employment programs, and their fellow executives are a mixture of racial backgrounds. Now their attitude of equality and respect between races is being undermined by their own son!

Some of us can only sigh when a loved one offers a remark or behaves in a way that is contrary to the beliefs we try to instill in our children. We might think it does no good or could cause more harm to confront that person. Or, more often, with young children we prefer to think the remark did not make much of an impression; the child will quickly forget it, and we'll cause damage by saying something and thereby calling attention to it.

If you think this, think again. The remark did not go unnoticed. It did make an impression. Damage is caused by letting it go by.

Let's look at the anecdote that opened this chapter. Beth realized that her mother's disturbing remark had made Sally concerned, but the easy distraction of the cupcakes led Beth to believe the girl's initial concern had immediately been forgotten. Challenging her mother could not only cause friction but would revive concern in Sally's mind.

We want to emphasize these points:

• Sally did not forget the remark. She might not dwell on it a minute later or even during the next few hours, but there is a very good chance that in bed that night she will hear her grandmother's voice and think about what she said. Certainly when she sees Denise at school on Monday, it will all come back to her.

• Children don't want to be in trouble themselves, and they get upset when friends are in trouble. Nana's remark implied that at some period in the future, Denise would be in trouble. Sally won't be satisfied until she knows what the trouble is and how Denise can avoid it.

• Though just two words, "those people" is a powerful expression. It immediately separates one race from another. And it's likely that the tone of voice was, at best, condescending, planting the seed in Sally's mind that one group of people is inferior to another.

• Because Sally loves and looks up to her grandmother, at least un-consciously the girl is prone to accept Nana's views. Even if it's only implied that something is wrong with Denise, this will taint their friendship: A small voice in Sally's mind will begin to ask, "What's wrong with her?" By extension, she could begin to be suspicious of all children she encounters who have visible racial differences.

• Even though she disapproved, by letting the remark slide Beth suggested it was appropriate. In a child's mind, if something is wrong, his or her parent is the first person to point it out and attempt to correct it.

What could Beth have done? And what can you do in a similar situation involving a loved one, especially a parent—weren't we taught to respect our elders?—that takes place in your home?

There are three responses we recommend. One is to challenge the remark immediately after it is uttered. No, we don't mean jump up and shout. Your child will be ill-served by a family feud and possibly frightened. The challenge could be a simple question, gently asked: "What do you mean by that?"

A follow-up question could be "Why do you feel that way?" This offers an opportunity for the loved one to describe how her views were formed, what her influences were. You can then point out that those views are no longer tenable and will certainly be unhelpful to your child's multiracial generation. If you're not sure how to dispute those influences, say that you want to find out the facts, and invite your child to explore them together with you. Emphasize that you're not challenging the loved one as a person, but that your attitudes are different and you would like to discuss the issue again when you've gathered more information.

This is a rather benign approach, but it makes clear to your child that you have serious doubts about a loved one's attitudes and will put in the effort to discover the truth.

Another approach is to prepare your child for attitudes loved ones may express. This is especially helpful for those of you whose relationship with a loved one is tenuous for other reasons; the last thing you need is a disagreement about race to further jeopardize the relationship.

There is before and after preparation. Discuss with your child before a visit what attitudes toward other racial groups a loved one has and, to the best of your knowledge, why he or she has those views. Even if you don't believe the attitudes are justified, explaining why and how they were formed teaches your child an understanding of other points of view—and by extension, tolerance. State that you don't agree with the attitudes and explain why you think it would be damaging to confront that person. It also helps to let your child know he or she is free to challenge remarks but must do so with a respectful attitude toward the loved one.

If you didn't prepare your child ahead of time and didn't challenge attitudes when they were expressed, it is vitally important after the loved one leaves that you sit down with your youngster and introduce the topic of differing racial attitudes. You are not confusing or upsetting your child. The absence of a follow-up discussion risks your child's forming his or her own conclusions without any indication that you object to what was expressed.

Clearly state your objections. Stress that you still love Grandpa or Aunt Helen but that you believe their attitudes about other racial groups are incorrect. Encourage your child to talk to you any time he or she encounters similar attitudes—from loved ones, at school, in the media.

We have urged this before and we will continue to urge it: You are your child's best and most influential source of information and support, and the line of communication must be open at all times.

A third approach is to refuse to allow a loved one to utter biased views—nip them in the bud! Sounds dictatorial, doesn't it? And there could be hell to pay. Suppose, in the first anecdote, that Beth knew from past experience what her mother was about to say. So Beth announces, "That's a condescending and hurtful remark, and I can see Sally was upset by it. I won't allow such things to be said in my home."

Fireworks, right? Years of therapy undone or soon to begin? Can you really say that to a parent, aunt, or brother?

We don't suggest you get on a soapbox and lecture relatives about the joys and advantages of racial understanding. (And no matter how enthusiastic you might be about this book, please don't use it as a weapon!) But often the reason why a family member utters condescending or bigoted remarks is that they have become a conversational habit, and they've become a habit because the host or hostess didn't make clear that they are unacceptable.

You can gracefully state that you object to such remarks being made, especially in front of your children, and then, having made your point, change the subject. Follow-up with your children is still a good idea, and at least they have seen that you disagreed in a firm manner with that sort of remark. In this case, the advantage of a pre-emptive strike is to assure that denigrating remarks are not made at all.

Do some of you feel more comfortable confronting family members than friends? It is often the case that we'll speak frankly to loved ones but are reluctant to endanger friendships. This is understandable: Blood ties make us feel more secure about the enduring quality of a relationship, while a relationship between friends doesn't have the same fundamental foundation.

A neighbor over for coffee might say, referring to a different racial group, "Oh, they're all on drugs" or "They're out to get us." The same degree of emotional attachment might not be there, but here in your child's home is an adult whose remarks carry some authority. Suppose you have an old friend from college visiting who has developed or retained racial stereotypes. At dinner she says, "The best thing to do is stay away from those people." Do you want to ruin the weekend or risk ending a longtime friendship because of a disagreement over race?

Yes and no.

Yes, in the sense that you have to consider your priorities. Is this friendship worth more than the healthy upbringing of your child? You might have to choose, but it's also possible you will find that your friendship can withstand the disagreement. Even if you can't have a meeting of minds, your friend realizes and accepts that the expression of certain attitudes is unwelcome in your home.

No, in the sense that friendships are important. They are a necessary component of a satisfying life. If you can't agree to disagree, then if your friendship is deep enough there should be room to forbid disagreeable attitudes being expressed in your home. This is true of neighbors, too. You can't control what goes on in their homes, but in yours, whether about politics or religion or race, your beliefs must be respected.

Are you thinking, "I can't do this"? Yes, you can. The healthy development of your children is at stake. And we think you'll find, more often than not, that people will respect your stand. They might feel uncomfortable themselves but will appreciate opposing points of view. Even if this doesn't happen, your youngsters will observe how you act on your beliefs.

Okay, you agree to try some or all of what we've suggested in your own home. What can you do about what happens in another's home? Your child has sleepovers in a neighbor's home, and there are times when she spends the weekend with Nana or an aunt and uncle. (Don't we long for these opportunities!) If we require that others respect what is permissible in our home, can we expect to control what goes on in someone else's home?

Not completely. But, again, you can prepare your child for unwholesome influences and be prepared afterwards to discuss with your child the attitudes presented to her.

Kelli Haley gladly accepted an invitation from her sister, Danielle, for her nine-year-old daughter, Charlene, to spend the night. Charlene and her eight-year-old cousin Jackie were good friends, and Kelli hoped they would grow up to be as close as she and her sister had always been.

When Charlene returns, she says she had a lot of fun, yet her mother can tell something has upset the girl. After some gentle questioning, Charlene reveals that when she and Jackie had put on jewelry and grown-up dresses, Aunt Danielle said they were cute, but then when they had added makeup that darkened their skin, Aunt Danielle said they looked like hookers and had them scrub it off immediately. Though Charlene didn't exactly know what hookers were, her aunt's tone of voice strongly indicated they were bad people.

Looking at her mother, Charlene asks, "Are girls with dark skin hookers?"

Startled, and at a loss for words, Kelli's only thought is to say no and change the subject. But after a few moments she realizes that if she avoids her daughter's question, Charlene would continue to wonder, and she herself would be reluctant in the future to allow Charlene to visit with Jackie.

How would you handle this dilemma? Remember, a nine-year-old is much more sophisticated than a younger child, and she won't be satisfied with a brush-off. Chances are you'll have to explain first what a hooker is! Once you've survived that, you should discuss how some people believe that women of color are more likely to be involved in prostitution. The facts do not support this, but it is an unpleasantly common perception, thanks in a large way to movies and TV shows.

As best she could, Kelli explained to her daughter that her aunt's reaction was wrong but that it doesn't mean her aunt felt bad about her. She assured Charlene she could stay with Jackie again and that she shouldn't worry about future insults.

The next day, Kelli called her sister and asked if she could come over for coffee. After catching up on family happenings, Kelli described her daughter's and her own feelings about Danielle labeling the girls hookers after they put on dark makeup. Danielle was flabbergasted. She never meant anything racial by it. It was the makeup on the girls' faces she objected to because it uncomfortably reminded her that Jackie was approaching adolescence. She admitted, however, that her perception of prostitutes was that most of them are blacks or Latinas.

Kelli invited her sister to join her on a research project to determine the racial composition of prostitutes. When both women stopped laughing, Danielle agreed that her comment gave an impression Kelli doesn't like. She would try to respect her sister's views and consider more carefully her own.

"I want these girls to continue to be best of friends," Kelli said, "in your home or mine. We have to work on this together."

Admittedly, the sisterly bond in the above anecdote strengthened a common objective—the continued companionship of cousins. But isn't it also true that many of us want our children to be friends with the children of our friends? As we mentioned earlier, we live in a mobile society, and often the friends we acquire in distant cities, suburbs, and villages are the closest we come to families. In the case of families that have experienced turmoil, friendships can be stronger and more desirable than family ties.

We aren't asking you to sacrifice friendships. We do ask you to keep uppermost in mind that your child and your friends' children comprise a generation that will be of diverse racial backgrounds. The accommodation you make today of avoiding or compromising the goal of cultural diversity will injure your child's chances of peaceful coexistence and benefiting from that diversity in the twenty-first century.

There's one other point we'd like to make: Is it worth it to create friction with a loved one over differing racial attitudes? Suppose you chose the course of confronting a loved one who has expressed a condescending or obviously biased attitude. Should your entire relationship be affected by that one difference of opinion?

Thankfully, very few of our emotional relationships are based on one aspect. We care about our parents, siblings, neighbors, and friends because they care about us, our needs, our common hopes, and our children. Across racial lines we are more alike than we are not: We want our children to grow up healthy, physically and psychologically, and to find a position in society that affords them sustenance and pride. Whatever his or her circumstances or color, no parent would hope for less.

It is the inherent strength in relationships between loved ones that allows for differences to exist and, over time, to be resolved. It is worth it to object to biased racial views being expressed in your home and to try to prevent your child from being subjected to unwholesome views in another's home. As important as this one aspect is, it should not taint your overall relationship with the people whom you care for and who care for you.

The bottom line is that by not saying or doing anything, you condone what was said or done. Silence should not be an option in your home. We urge you to take the long view: Will you do what is necessary now to prepare your child for the rainbow generation?

Part II

The World Beyond Your Walls

6
Making the Grade

Your child has reached school age. This is an exciting time but also a painful one: Even if you've been the best parents since the Cleavers or the Huxtables, from now on you will not be the sole focus of your child's life.

For one of the authors, escorting his daughter to her first day of kindergarten was a wrenching experience, with powerful emotions being sorted out. He realized she was "not my baby anymore" with a heightened awareness of his own mortality (even though she was only five!) and the sense that increasingly she would be exposed to a wide variety of new influences. His fervent hope was that if any of those influences were troublesome or involved racism, she would turn to her parents for help.

Inevitably, some of the influences involve prejudice. No matter how hard you have worked in your home to foster an open-minded atmosphere and an appreciation of others, you can't control the world beyond your walls. For at least the next decade, the school environment will have a profound impact on your child's life. And more than at any other time in history, that environment has to find ways to address multicultural issues and interaction.

Why are the 1990s such a crucial turning point? As we mentioned in Chapter 1, a study of American public schools released in 1991 revealed that, by 1995, 34 percent of students will be nonwhite. One of the authors of the study was quoted in the *New York Times* as saying, "It's more dramatic than most people realize. Most people have a sense that this is occurring but don't realize how rapidly the changes are taking place and how dramatic the changes are."

In some areas, the changes are clearly evident. For example, as of 1992, 83 percent of students in the San Francisco public school system were nonwhite. In the Los Angeles public school system, two-thirds of the students are Latino.

Parents living outside of major urban areas might think their schools will not undergo significant demographic change. They should think again. While the change might not be as rapid, every school system in the country is seeing an increase in students of color.

Parents have several issues to consider: Is my child's school prepared to teach a changing student body? Will it adequately prepare my child to succeed in a changing society? Will my good intentions and teaching of acceptance be undermined by the school? Should I get involved in the school or leave the curriculum to the professionals? If my child does not receive a multicultural education, is she being robbed of a wonderful opportunity to learn about the global society of the twenty-first century?

Parents of nonwhite students have additional concerns. Many of the teachers and administrators our children will encounter are our age or older and thus, like us, grew up in a less enlightened racial climate. The effects of even very subtle prejudice on students of color have been well documented. Even some professionals believe that these students are intellectually inferior to their white peers. So a primary concern is: Is the school environment progressive and flexible enough to provide my child with an education that is as enriching as that offered to white children?

One other consideration for parents is that participation in school inevitably means children will undergo the pull of peers. Some studies have shown that children are more likely to be influenced by fellow students than by their teachers. So you have to deal not only with the attitudes and practices of school personnel but with the baggage of bias that children from other homes are carrying into the classroom. (We discuss this in more detail in Chapter 8.)

Whatever misgivings they have, many parents send their children off to school with some relief. As we have mentioned, parenting is an exhausting occupation. On top of caring for children and being on call twenty-four hours a day, a lot of parents work outside the home. The burden is even greater in single-parent households. So when the child enters school and is occupied for six or more hours a day, we feel at least a sense of temporary freedom; we can now focus on other areas of our life.

Unfortunately, some parents allow this time to be an opportunity to abdicate responsibility. "My kid's old enough, I pay taxes (or tuition), it's their turn to take care of him!" After-school programs and extracurricular activities offer even more time away from home. Some parents would rather hear from the school only when there's a problem; otherwise, let the school do its job. Race relations are one issue often allowed to fall into this gap.

We have urged you to take a few moments to look in the mirror and evaluate your own racial attitudes. Now we urge you to think about the school environment that in a big way will affect your youngster's outlook. What is the racial composition of the student body? of the faculty? How much does it teach about other cultures, and what does it teach? How does the administration handle racial conflicts, and how quick is it to label conflicts as race-related? What are individual teachers' attitudes toward various cultural groups?

If you don't know the answers to these questions, you are taking a risk that what your child learns will conflict with your attitudes toward a multicultural society. Keep in mind that, especially in elementary school, children absorb vast amounts of information. Just as with reading, writing, and 'rithmetic, what your children learn at this stage forms a foundation upon which the rest of their lives are built.

Warren, a second-grader, enjoyed school and really liked Ms. Kelso, his teacher. She read fun stories, she was physically affectionate, and it was okay if he got an answer wrong, because she helped him figure out the right answer and never criticized. Even when a classmate misbehaved, she didn't yell; Ms. Kelso took the child aside and gently calmed him down.

But Warren was curious about something. Every Friday there was a quiz on the words they had learned that week. Sometimes Warren and a few others in the class wrote the spelling words quickly, and Ms. Kelso patted them on the head and stuck stars on their papers. Yet when some students finished early, Ms. Kelso said, "You can't be done already. You'd better look over the words again and make sure they're right." These classmates were almost always Enrico, Jasmine, and Noel, students of color. Ms. Kelso must know what she was doing. Those kids probably didn't learn the words and just wanted to get the test over with.

Ms. Kelso would likely be shocked to be told she was singling out students of color, and in any case she might think the class didn't notice. She could even offer a reasonable explanation. But children respond to the concrete realities they perceive, not to abstract explanations. Warren observed classmates different from himself being treated as intellectually inferior.

What else do children observe even in a school environment whose official policy is racial understanding, sensitivity, and acceptance? Here are a few examples:

• It's time to cast the first-grade school play. This year it's *The Princess and the Pea.* Allison is chosen to be the princess, and Charles wants to be the prince. But the teacher suggests that Charles play one of the servants and gives the part of the prince to Frank. The teacher thought she was avoiding potential friction: Would Allison's parents appreciate having their daughter play opposite a boy of Asian descent? Or would it confuse students that the illustration in the book they were using for the play clearly showed the prince to be Caucasian, not Asian?

• Eight-year-old Jim shows up for basketball tryouts. He plays well and thinks he has an excellent chance of being selected for the team. But the coach doesn't pick him. Jim notices that the team has only black players. When Jim musters up the courage to ask the coach why he wasn't chosen, the coach replies, "Hey, you did really well, but you guys are not the athletes these other guys are." Feeling hurt and angry, Jim consoles himself by thinking that sports is the only thing black kids can do well. The coach might realize he's resorted to a stereotype but believes it's okay because it's a positive one.

• When studying American history, Steven is proud to learn about Washington, Jefferson, Lincoln, and Teddy Roosevelt. But a black classmate, David, keeps waiting for a mention of the great figures like Frederick Douglass and George Washington Carver that his parents had told him about. When he asks the teacher, she replies, "Well, none of your people were presidents or founded this country." David feels humiliated, and Steven observes him being teased by his classmates.

• Henrietta's family arrived from Cuba only two years ago. Yet the second-grader has quickly learned English and she seems to have a special aptitude for math. Still, when the teacher calls on her, she bows her head before delivering her answer. One day the teacher exclaims in frustration, "What's the matter with you? Why can't you look at me when I talk to you!" Henrietta is crushed that her revered teacher is angry with her. The teacher didn't understand that in some Latino cultures, looking down is a sign of respect.

Hopefully, even though your child is in another environment for much of every day, he will come to you when he's troubled by a race-related problem. How do you handle this? Obviously, common sense is essential. As with any issue, keep the lines of communication open. We don't suggest aggressive prying—children, too, deserve their own space—but ask questions. And don't just ask questions that call for only positive answers. Inquire if anything occurred at school that made your child uncomfortable. Ask open-ended questions instead of ones that can be answered with yes or no.

While respect for teachers is important, don't automatically assert that a teacher is always right and say things like "I don't know how she puts up with you kids." If your child can't talk with you about what bothers her, she will turn to peers, and some peers may have been brought up with a closed-minded view of other cultures.

Being in school should not mean that your child's education ends at dismissal time. If you think the curriculum does not offer enough cultural diversity, supplement it with books and activities. Most libraries today have children's books featuring characters of various racial backgrounds, and many magazines and local newspapers report events involving other races. (Please look for the positive articles and photographs beyond the bias incidents.)

Purchase or borrow a cookbook of a particular culture and periodically try a different recipe. Food is universal (every human has to eat), and demonstrating how different cultures eat is a subtle yet effective way of not only appreciating differences but showing how alike people are.

Encourage your child to correspond with a pen pal from another country. YMCAs, foreign embassies, cultural institutions, UNICEF, and other organizations usually have eager pals available. Your youngster gets to practice her reading and writing, and in a fun way learns about how other people live. If your child is a little older, you can try hosting a foreign-exchange student. Imagine your child and her new friend trading clothing and learning each other's language!

It is extremely important that you encourage your child to empathize when he reports that a classmate was made to feel bad because of his race. Young children are already sensitive to the hurting of peers, so you don't want your youngster to wallow in another's pain, but you do want him to understand a classmate was treated unfairly and that maybe he can make a special effort to be a friend. If the effort is rebuffed, point out that it probably wasn't because of racial differences but because the other child might not be ready to open up to a peer and perhaps is being comforted by his own parents.

What you don't want to do, if your child has observed prejudice or has been the victim of it, is nothing. We're not perfect, and sometimes we don't know how best to respond. But thinking the problem will go away on its own is like telling a child with nightmares that the monster in the closet will disappear if the door is kept closed. Talking about the problem at school, even if you feel inadequate, lets your youngster know you are concerned and will be an ally in finding an answer.

It is an enormous advantage in the battle against prejudice when the people on the front lines in the education system, the teachers, are ready, willing, and able to address problems and especially go that extra mile to take note of and mitigate potential problems.

Diane Soriano teaches second grade at a suburban school. After reading to her class a story about space exploration, she asked the class to do a project on the subject of space. The next day the youngsters came in with model spaceships, drawings, and planets made of Play-Doh. One white child, June, wrote a three-page play called *The Friendly Space Creature*.

Members of the class began to perform the play. But one part of it caught Diane's attention. When the space creature appears to two characters, one asks, "Is it a friendly space creature?" The other replies, "Look at its skin. If it has dark skin it's bad. If it doesn't, it's friendly."

Diane stopped herself from halting the play at that point, though she was concerned about the African American, Middle Eastern, and Latino students in her class. Afterward she took June aside and asked her, "Why would dark skin make the space creature bad?" June shrugged and replied, "I just wrote it that way."

Diane was a believer in artistic freedom, but she suspected an unconscious bias. She asked June's parents to see her, and she explained her concern.

The parents were surprised and at first couldn't explain their daughter's choice of color. But as they talked further, they offered that recently they had watched a couple of science-fiction videos, and the villains were dressed in black and wore dark masks. Diane pointed out that a problem could develop with June's associating evil with dark colors and that, without positive intervention, their daughter could convey that feeling toward dark-skinned peers. The parents promised to talk to June and to serve as race-conscious editors of future literary efforts.

In this anecdote, the teacher immediately got involved and worked with the parents, who otherwise were unaware of the media's effect on their child. Unfortunately, not every teacher has his or her antennae up for bias signals.

We're reminded of an unpleasant lesson taught to first-grade students at a suburban Pennsylvania school in January 1993. To demonstrate how slaves were once sold, the teacher had the only two black youngsters in her class come to the front of the room and pretend they were slaves on an auction block. One of the students reported that "the teacher acted like she was selling us" and that she would be sold for "about $10 as a house cleaner." The demonstration also showed how slaves were chained to a post before being flogged. Ironically, the incident came to light that evening at a meeting of parents, teachers, and administrators who had gathered to discuss ways to improve race relations in the school system.

Except when it comes to salaries, in most communities teachers are viewed to have an exalted position. They are well educated, have patience with our rambunctious youngsters, and are responsible for intellectual stimulation and growth.

But teachers are like you and me. They have families, shop at the local stores, try to pay mortgages or rents on time, would love to win the lottery, get viruses and toothaches, own cars that break down, swoon over Mel Gibson and Denzel Washington, Joan Chen and Maria Conchita Alonso, or A. Alvarez, and have acquired certain attitudes toward other races. Most work very hard to hide these biases or are unaware that they possess them. Many of them, alas, have never been trained how to teach children of diverse backgrounds—they simply find themselves confronted with the situation.

What should schools be doing to prepare your child for a multicultural society? We have several recommendations:

• Require teachers and administrators to take at least one course, and preferably several courses over time, on cultural and racial sensitivity. Some organizations and government agencies offer courses free of charge, but if there is a cost, the few extra dollars on your annual tax bill are worth it.

• Immediately alter the wall space of classrooms. We support drawings and photographs of George Washington, Abraham Lincoln, and the Wright Brothers taking off at Kitty Hawk. But there should also be portraits of Martin Luther King, Booker T. Washington, Cesar Chavez, Frederick Douglass, Barbara Jordan, Sitting Bull, Benjamin Banneker (a black inventor who helped plan the nation's capital), Richard Wright, Rosa Parks, and Amy Tan, as well as illustrations of people of color who were responsible for such advances as blood plasma, open-heart surgery, the phonograph, the fountain pen, the traffic light, and the baby crib. Without these daily reminders, students are likely to believe that only white people were responsible for the society, implements, arts, and institutions we know today.

• Make sure that the school routinely celebrates the accomplishments and features of other cultures. You might think, "Well, we celebrate Black History Month." This is a positive step, but it's only a first step and possibly a misleading step.

It is beneficial to students of European heritage to experience a month in which African American history and contributions are celebrated. Think back to when we were students: Was this ever done? Today's students are offered information that simply wasn't previously presented or was presented in what amounts to a footnote.

The risk is that the exposure to those contributions will end when February does. This gives the misleading impression that black contributions to America are confined to a small area. And, with very few exceptions, schools do not have months devoted to celebrating the cultures of Asians, Latinos, and Native Americans.

• Look into how truly multicultural your school's curriculum is. An occasional reference by teachers or textbooks to the contributions to America of people of color has the same impact as adding a teaspoon of water to a recipe—does it really influence the flavor?

In geography, is there any emphasis on other parts of the world? In science, are the inventions and integral research of people of color given full credit? In history, is the only mention of blacks associated with slavery? The curriculum must include, with the proper proportionate weight, the positive impact of African Americans and various immigrant groups. Does it teach that much of our transcontinental railroad system was constructed by the sweat and blood of Asians?

There has been a criticism of some multicultural education programs: They have been dubbed a "tourist curriculum." This label pertains to displays of clothing, food, and other surface aspects of different cultures (say, at holidays). Critics charge this is patronizing, emphasizing the exotic differences between cultures and avoiding the real-life daily experiences and problems of different people. Children visit these cultures and then go home without having learned that the people around them really do live and breathe these cultures. Some exposure is better than none, but we do urge schools to present to all students on a daily basis the various threads that now comprise our national fabric.

• Carefully examine the textbooks. Since the previous generation, great strides have been made in incorporating non-Europeans' influence on American history and culture. But many textbooks have not gone far enough, and in thousands of school districts across the country textbooks are used that were written a decade or more ago.

Every day, students are assigned to read portions of these textbooks, and much of the learning they retain through life comes from them. It is likely a textbook assigned in eleventh or twelfth grade will not leave the same impression as one used in second or fourth grade.

• Teachers should offer opportunities for interracial groupings of students to work on assignments. Why? Studies have shown that dividing a class into small racially and ethnically diverse groups to pursue assignments fosters mutual interdependence and interest in a common goal. Children go beyond surface differences toward cooperation. Parents should also investigate whether classroom seating arrangements are isolating certain youngsters and "just happen" to conform to racial groups.

• How do school personnel handle name calling? In even the most progressive schools, youngsters insult each other using racial epithets. Punishing a child is counterproductive—he feels resentful and vows to just be less obvious next time. School personnel must (a) look beyond the incident—such as an argument—to what caused the friction between the children, and explain that their races had nothing to do with it, (b) contact the parents to let them know their child is expressing anger or frustration by using denigrating racial remarks, and (c) provide forums for learning about and improving race relations (guest speakers, discussion groups, role models).

• Think about what constitutes disruptive behavior. In the early grades, some teachers can be irritated by the "clingyness" of some black children and how they are quick to answer questions while white students patiently wait their turn. These are not examples of bad behavior. Studies have shown that for some African Americans child rearing is very much hands-on and demonstrative and that much of black culture is influenced by the church, which includes a lot of verbal call-and-response in its services and activities. Of course, we must remember that black people are not monolithic and black children do not all behave the same. Many black children are raised to be quiet, "seen and not heard," while others are raised to be more active.

In later grades, some school personnel can be irritated or even intimidated by the behavior of students of any color, not understanding that this behavior is based on their culture and is not intended to be disruptive or disrespectful. And personnel might be too quick to label incidents as racially motivated if people of different races are involved. Teachers and administrators, especially those who have not undergone sensitivity training, should be willing to consider other factors beside and beyond skin color. Otherwise there is the risk that the participants in the dispute will believe their racial differences are the problem.

• What is the racial composition of faculty and the administration? Seeing teachers and authority figures of different backgrounds working together sends a strong message to students.

• Private schools must make an extra effort to racially diversify the student body. No matter how good the quality of education is or the emphasis placed on other cultures, children will emerge from a private school with a disadvantage if they have not interacted on a daily basis with youngsters of other races.

Active recruiting of these youngsters is necessary, and if the tuition is a prohibitive factor, for some students many private schools now offer scholarships. This might raise tuition costs, but it's worth the extra dollars to provide all children with a culturally enriched educational experience. It is unfair and potentially damaging to your child to have him wait until high school or even college before encountering peers from other racial backgrounds.

Even though your child is in school, we're turning to you: Get involved! Aside from concerns about prejudice, you should be involved because you want to shape the education system your child will grow up in. Think about it: You send your youngster off to kindergarten at age five, and when she emerges from school she's eighteen. You can't just entrust such a substantial part of her life to others, can you?

Certainly not. And just as in this age range your child will go from learning how to spell "lamp" to computing the light-years to the farthest observable galaxy (which we couldn't do!), she will form an indelible impression of people with different racial backgrounds. This can't be left solely to the school system. As with any educational issue, push the system to reflect your views.

One way is direct action. Most schools set aside evenings for parent-teacher conferences. While these are opportunities, they represent only skirmishes. The inundated teacher has dozens of parents to meet, and the conversations usually consist of what has already happened. We urge you to make specific appointments with your child's teacher, and separately with the principal, to discuss the curriculum content and his or her attitudes toward other racial groups. It is unlikely you will be told, "I hate ————!" and most school personnel don't consciously feel that way. But body language, tone of voice, objective discussion of curriculum, and subtle implications will indicate if your child is receiving an open-minded and culturally diverse education.

Indirect action, which ultimately has a direct effect, can be helpful too. Join or be more involved in your school's PTA or PTO. With an energetic membership, these organizations do much more than hold bake sales and conduct raffles (a common misperception). If your parent-teacher organization presents a platform of promoting multicultural education and the school administration doesn't respond accordingly, go to the school board. Why? In many communities, school boards represent the basic foundation of our democratic system. Its members and its budgets are voted in or out. The PTA can strongly influence the outcome of elections. So making your feelings known will have an effect—or change the leadership!

Individually, volunteer to make a presentation to your child's class. This is especially effective in the lower grades. Your child will be proud, and his classmates will be impressed. Read an African, Latino, or Asian folktale—anything coming from you will carry extra weight.

Contact an organization that can place information, programs, and other resources at your disposal. Among the possibilities are the National Committee for Citizens in Education, 800-638-9675 (800-532-9832 in Spanish); the Alliance for Parental Involvement in Education, 518-392-6900; the Institute for Responsive Education, 617-353-3309; the National PTA, 312-787-8342; and the National Education Association Professional Library, 800-229-4200.

Supervise your child's homework. You might do this anyway to judge if it is too advanced or regressive, but take note of the attention paid to cultural diversity. If you think it's biased toward one racial group, arrange to talk to the teacher. He or she may completely agree with your concern yet be unaware that the assignments did not offer enough access to other cultures.

Look for signs that your child is being subjected to prejudice. This is delicate. We don't want you to be overly concerned or suspicious, but you must be attentive. Does he seem unusually quiet when he returns from school? Has she withdrawn from school-related activities? Is his performance in school declining? Lowered self-esteem is a sure signal that your child is experiencing a serious problem. It might not have anything to do with prejudice, but you really can't ignore this possibility. Ask your child first, and if she's reluctant to talk, see her teacher.

One other very important topic is choosing the school your child will attend. Of course, many parents don't have a choice; they send their children to the local public school. Yet some parents who strongly support multiculturalism might choose to move into communities that have public schools with mixed-race compositions. Due to the transient nature of modern life, many families with school-age children relocate one or more times, and the school is an important factor in determining the community to live in.

Some parents who have taken the extra step of placing their children in a multiracial public school are disappointed when it seems their best intentions have gone awry. Their children might report fights at school attributed to racial differences or the parents might become deeply concerned that the quality of education is declining. They might think, "Should we move or try to put our kids in a private school?"

We urge parents to stick with it. One reason is that by abandoning the school you send a message to your child that it's better to run from problems than to resolve them. And as time goes on, the memory your child retains of associating with peers of other races will be an unpleasant one, likely to leave an undercurrent of fear.

Consider several alternative actions:

• Work with administrators, teachers, and other parents to create a more harmonious environment. The school can form multiracial groups of students who can talk about their differences and frustrations.

• Encourage your child to have contact outside the school with classmates of other races.

• With administrators, focus on the root cause of incidents in the school. While they might have evolved into a racial issue, with peers taking sides based on skin color, often conflicts arise out of problems that initially have nothing to do with race. Also try to ascertain the sensitivity level of administrators and teachers: Are they too quick to label conflicts as racially based?

• Keep in mind that concern for quality of education is not confined to any one racial group. Black parents want high standards as well as Asian, Latino as well as Caucasian. If the school is subpar, all parents should address the reasons and develop solutions.

• Don't assume your child wants out! In our practice we receive many calls from youngsters expressing concern over racial tension who want advice on how to work through problems, not avoid them.

• If you do decide to switch schools or move to another community, find other ways—clubs, sports teams, informal gatherings—to put your child in contact with other races. If you don't replace one multiracial environment with another one, your child will always think things didn't work out because of racial incompatibility.

• Without exposure to cultural diversity, students who attend private institutions during the elementary and middle school years often have difficulty adjusting to the more diverse environment of high school, college, or society as a whole. A private school curriculum should include study of many cultures, and there should be financial or other incentives to ensure that youngsters of all races are enrolled.

Fortunately, many schools in the United States are turning to embracing other cultures. Administrators and faculty realize the demographic tide is turning and that they must either ride the wave or get washed under into irrelevance and obsolescence. While there are some rotten apples, the educational barrel is full of well-meaning, intelligent people who feel a calling to teach and nurture the next generation the best ways they can.

Many educators are going above and beyond their calling. We offer one example: A few years ago Finley Junior High School in Huntington, New York, formed a Multicultural Action Committee, known as MAC. Founded by English teacher Lisa Eskin, it not only brings children of diverse backgrounds together for social and educational activities but has an adoption program in which black, Latino, and Asian students adopt each other as brothers and sisters so they can experience each other's family histories, customs, and attitudes.

The student and faculty participants stay in each other's homes and exchange clothes so that they learn about different cultures. Teachers set the example by walking down the hallways in borrowed clothing and speaking the languages they are learning.

"We try not to preach, except to say we're all Americans, and we do have to respect and accept our differences," Eskin says. "The fact that some of the MAC kids don't ordinarily join clubs indicates we've tapped into a fundamental desire among young people to coexist."

Eskin adds:

> Schools can't wait to let kids make up their own minds about racism. We have got to get in there and at least provide an opportunity to understand we're not born prejudiced; we acquire biases. And the way society is shaping up, all of us will be much better off and enjoy life more if we don't carry the baggage of bias.

Brown v. Board of Education, the unanimous U.S. Supreme Court decision in 1954, provided the legal foundation for the racial integration of public schools. Almost forty years later, children of many races sit side by side in the classroom, but physical proximity in the school environment does not by itself ensure appreciation between racial groups.

Our schools must become culturally integrated. This isn't a political call to action, though some readers may see it as such. The bottom-line question is, What's in it for you—the parent, the teacher, the caregiver? The chance to raise and nurture a child who can prosper intellectually, culturally, and emotionally in connection with a twenty-first-century society that represents the cumulative effect of hundreds of years of diversity.

Please don't be complacent and suppose that the schools by themselves will resolve their racial problems and progressively prepare your child for a global society. One sad example of lingering prejudice among people who should know better: In July 1992, the school board in Westfield, Massachusetts, debated a proposal to ban from first- and second-grade classrooms any teacher who spoke English with an accent. The leading supporter of the proposal was the city's mayor! Fortunately, the school board rejected the proposal.

Your schools can prepare or they can deny. Will you leave the choice up to chance?

7

The Media and the Message

Two white youngsters, Gary and Seth, both eight, are busily biking up and down the street where Gary lives. Finally, Seth skids to a stop on the sidewalk in front of Gary's house and says, "I'm dying of thirst. Got anything to drink?"

"No one's home, but I'm sure it's okay to have what's in the fridge," Gary replies.

The boys find a large container of apple juice, and after filling their glasses, they flop down into chairs in the living room. Gary picks up the remote control and idly changes channels on the TV.

"Not much on, huh?" Seth remarks.

"Nope. Cartoons are for babies, and this stuff"—Gary gestures toward a soap opera scene—"yecch, all they do is kiss or fight. Hey, wait a minute!" Gary picks up another remote, this one for the VCR. "My Dad must've been watching this last night. Let's see what it is."

When the video begins, the boys see it is an action picture. Seth mentions that his parents had seen this in a movie theater, and that they said it was pretty good—about the police chasing a gang of crooks to recover some super-duper device. The opening scenes show the inside of an office building.

"Look there, I bet he's one of the crooks," Gary announces.

Seth sees a man who has just entered the bank. "If you haven't seen this, how do you know already?" he asks his friend.

"Look and listen, dummy. He's a spic. That means in this movie he's either a pimp, a drug dealer, or he's going to whack somebody's head off with a machete." Gary adds, "What's the matter? Don't you pay attention when you watch videos?"

Seth thought he did, but he'd never picked up on this information about Latino characters, which Gary was so certain about. Well, he'd know better next time. Seth settles down in the chair, waiting for the crook with the brown skin and accent to whip out a machete.

It would be nice to report that Gary's comment was completely off-base and that the youngster was putting into the video a prejudice learned only from his parents. Unfortunately, it is all too often true that the media offers unflattering (and worse) portrayals of people of color.

Whether we approve or not, the fact is, children are strongly influenced by what the media presents. After parents (and sometimes extended family) and the education system, the information gathered from a screen or printed page has the greatest impact on the values youngsters acquire. Their imaginations are sparked by what they read, or have read to them, and what they see in moving pictures. Much of their play involves acting out what they have read or imitating what they have seen.

In an ideal world, exposure to media would reinforce the values imparted by parents and teachers. In our society, however, especially with racial stereotypes, images in the media can and often do contradict efforts to promote an appreciation of and respect for various racial groups.

Of course, there have been significant changes over the years. Just as TV shows in the 1950s and 1960s blithely conveyed gender stereotypes (think of the moms in "Leave It to Beaver" and "Father Knows Best"), they relied on racial stereotypes for humor and suspense. Many of us can recall eye-rolling characters like Rochester on "The Jack Benny Show," the inept savages in "Tarzan" (one episode in 1966 had Diana Ross and the Supremes as nuns in Africa), the evil and equally inept Native Americans in "Wagon Train" and "Rawhide," and the tortured linguistics of elevator operator Jose Jimenez. Also, many shows did not feature people of color at all or only in the most inconsequential roles, implying they were not really part of normal American society.

Today, it is still possible to encounter TV characters who are descendants of Amos and Andy or Stepin' Fetchit on nightly sitcoms. As recently as 1992 there was a sitcom called "Teech" that was filled with jokes about lawn jockeys and watermelon eating.

The good news is that network executives are placing more shows featuring black characters on TV. According to a survey done in the fall of 1992, of the seventy-four prime-time entertainment series on the four networks, twelve featured largely black casts, more than any time previously. Alas, all twelve are comedies. Dramas featuring black actors in the majority of roles are rare. By watching TV, viewers would not—with few exceptions—get the impression that there is a black middle class, or any segment of African American life, that struggles to deal with everyday issues like child rearing, intimacy, and career goals.

There seems to have been more progress in the movies, with several African American actors attracting a healthy slice of the audience. Among them are Danny Glover, Whoopi Goldberg, Denzel Washington, Morgan Freeman, Lou Gossett, Jr., Larry Fishburne, Wesley Snipes, Halle Berry, and Whitney Houston.

Compare these inroads to a generation ago, when the only people of color to garner a popular following were Bill Cosby on "I Spy" and Diahann Carroll on "Julia" in TV and Sidney Poitier in the movies. Spike Lee, Bill Duke, Wayne Wang, Matt Rich, and the Hudlin brothers head a growing list of nonwhite filmmakers who are consistently reaching a widespread audience, when a generation ago there were only the occasional and isolated efforts by Ossie Davis, Gordon Parks, and Melvin Van Peebles.

Popular culture is different, but not different enough. When you consider the changing demographics, particularly the rapidly growing Latino and Asian populations, isn't it odd that these groups receive little representation on TV and in the movies?

People of color can be found in some supporting roles. But even so, many of these roles portray African Americans as violent criminals and clownish, Latinos as pimps and drug dealers, Asians as sneaky and amoral, and Native Americans as drunken or self-destructively noble savages.

The result is that despite your best efforts to instill in your youngster, whatever his or her race, an appreciation of people of other backgrounds, the influence of the media either undermines those efforts or provides weak support.

Let's look at television first, simply because most children are exposed to this form of media more than any other. Some studies report that the average American child spends as much as six hours per day in front of a TV, more time than is spent doing homework, reading, playing outdoors, and interacting with parents. The TV has become America's babysitter, especially in homes where both parents are away for most of the day or there is only one parent.

Younger children enjoy watching cartoons because the images move fast, there is a lot of slapstick and other amusing ingredients, and invariably they have happy endings. They fuel imaginations, and indeed several successful filmmakers today, such as Steven Spielberg, cite cartoons as having had a stimulating effect on their creativity and visual abilities.

Today's cartoon makers are more careful not to rely on stereotypes and to present different-colored characters. But the airwaves are flooded with cartoons made many years ago. Our own parents grew up watching Bugs Bunny, Popeye, Daffy Duck, Woody Woodpecker, and other popular figures of fun. The proliferation of cable TV means a hunger for programming, and in the area of cartoons, because there simply are not enough being produced now to satisfy that hunger, TV stations have emptied the vaults of cartoons made as far back as fifty years ago.

If you don't already allow yourself this guilty pleasure, sit down and watch an hour or two of cartoons. You will see "bad" characters often presented as dark- and yellow-skinned or speaking with accents. Some cartoons contain musical interludes, which sometimes include dancing darkies doing exaggerated minstrel shows. These cartoons reflect the attitudes of society a generation or more ago, when it was routine and expedient to offer villains and silly characters as nonwhite.

For various reasons—most of them economic—these older cartoons are becoming more prevalent. One example is the twenty-four-hour cable cartoon network that began broadcasting in October 1992. The operator, Turner Television, owns the rights to all the MGM cartoons made decades ago and licenses others from the same period. (The network only recently banned one cartoon called "Jungle Jitters" because of the derogatory caricatures.) Short of leaving the TV off, your young child won't escape these cartoons.

Older children watch live-action shows, with or without you. In the early evening, most of these shows are sitcoms. Again, take a good look at them. The fact that your child actually sees a black family on the screen is a positive development. (In the 1950s there was only one noncomedic show on TV that starred a black performer, "The Nat

King Cole Show"; it was canceled after one season for lack of sponsorship.) Yet quite a few of today's TV characters still have buffoonish elements, and the fact that they are in comedies removes them a bit from reality. (Children who do not otherwise have exposure to black families might think all of their homes contain laugh tracks!) And again, there is no visual exposure to other nonwhite family situations.

With dramatic shows, try to think of one with a contemporary setting featuring people of color in prominent roles. Other than "I'll Fly Away," which, as of this writing, has been moved to public television, there isn't one. There are certainly no Latino or Asian equivalents of "thirtysomething" that show people of color coping with everyday concerns.

Putting entertainment aside, we might believe that at least news programming accurately reflects our changing society. Well, there are some problems here, too. News shows and documentaries are overly eager to portray people of color when reporting on social ills. Here is an excerpt from an opinion piece on network news shows by the novelist and poet Ishmael Reed, published in the April 9, 1991, issue of the *New York Times:*

> *These programs are the chief source of information that Americans receive about the world. More often than not, they associate black and Hispanic people exclusively with drugs, crime, unwed parenthood, welfare, homelessness, child abuse and rape, although the majority of the people involved in these circumstances are white. . . .*
>
> *[A] USA Today poll showed that 15 percent of the drug users in America are black, while 70 percent are white. According to Black Entertainment News, however, television news associates drugs with blacks 50 percent of the time, while only 32 percent of the drug stories focus on whites.*
>
> *[Last month] NBC and CNN used blacks exclusively to illustrate Justice Department statistics about both black and white crime. On NBC's report, a white family was used to show the vulnerability of Americans to crime.*

One of the authors had a similar experience: On TV a few years ago there was a Bill Moyers documentary about an inner-city New Jersey neighborhood near the one in which the author grew up. Poverty abounded and everyone interviewed—drug dealers, addicts, high school dropouts, welfare recipients, angry renters, single mothers, and unemployed of all ages—were black. No mention was made of black middle and professional classes. The author's gang of friends who grew up in the area had gone on to become a physician, a lawyer, a journalist, and a clinical psychologist. Doubtlessly, viewers received the impression that the entire black population of the area was barely clinging to civilization. Would there have been a similar lack of representation in a documentary about a white neighborhood?

Most executives at news organizations are white, middle-aged males. The views presented are skewed accordingly, to the detriment of people of color as well as of women. And as Ishmael Reed contended, these views comprise the main source of information Americans receive.

Suppose you conclude that it's best to avoid TV. You're going to rely on the print media, books and magazines. And even before you impart their information to your children, you will absorb some of it.

Again, most major magazines and newspapers have very few African Americans, Asians, and Latinos as decision makers. Editors don't necessarily intend to present biased views, but inevitably the lack of racial diversity on mastheads results in biased presentations to the reading public.

One example occurred in 1991. *Newsweek* magazine did a cover story on the increase in bank robberies. Statistics in the article clearly pointed out that the vast majority of bank robbers were white. However, the photographs accompanying the text showed only black perpetrators. Given that a picture is worth a thousand words, these photos overwhelmed the paragraph or two of statistics in the article and gave readers the wrong impression.

Granted, your children are unlikely to depend on newspapers and magazines for their views of the world. You're reading them stories at bedtime and they're buying comic books for fun reading. Please take a few moments and objectively consider the content of the stories you read to your child, especially fairy tales.

With very few exceptions, the fairy tales that have remained popular to the present day offer light-skinned or brightly clothed characters as good, and dark-skinned or dark-clothed characters as evil. Bad characters, such as witches, are associated with dark colors in "Cinderella," "Snow White," and many tales collected by the Grimm brothers. We still read these stories because of the positive moral messages they impart, but think about the subtle messages they also convey about color.

Most of the popular fairy tales are from Europe and were written or collected in the seventeenth and eighteenth centuries, and they reflect the prejudices of that place and time. By no means do they reflect worldwide culture and attitudes. In Chinese folk tales, evil characters often appear dressed in white; Armenians associate death with light blue, and Egyptians, with yellow; and in some other cultures, people with red hair are viewed as sinister.

Contemporary children's literature is more progressive, but there are still subtle, perhaps unintended, messages. Recently one of the authors was reading a story to his four-year-old son about a woman who, while scavenging for useful items on a beach, finds a corked bottle. A voice inside pleads to loosen the cork. She does, and a creature emerges. It claims to be extraordinarily evil, and the woman asks that it prove how fearsome it can become. In the succeeding pages the creature grows in size and turns darker in color until it is a huge black reptile. This book was published in 1987.

Have you taken a look in your child's school library or the children's room of your local library? Again, many wonderful books are available, but there is an equal or greater amount of books written a number of years ago when there was little sensitivity about color associations. Despite their stereotype, many librarians are well-educated, informed people who eschew bias, yet they also operate within budgets that force them to offer shelves stocked with books that are racially unenlightened. We'll wager someone with a library card can still procure *Little Black Sambo.*

Comic books have a strong influence on young imaginations. Children identify with superheroes. When playing, they often imitate the powers and personalities of various costumed crusaders. Up until recently, under the disguises most of the superheroes were white and the bad guys were dressed in dark colors. To adults, this might seem too simplistic to make a lasting impression. But remember, your children are very impressionable, and unconsciously they will equate good and evil with light and dark colors, and in a subtle way that "colors" their views of the people they encounter in real life. Some children of color generalize to people and internalize these negative images.

In comic books as well as other reading material available to children, the marked absence of nonwhite characters (except in minor, supporting roles) sends a message too: These people are not an important part of society. Even if a child escapes the association with evil, there is the impression that people different from herself exist only on the periphery of society. As we've discussed, twenty-first-century demographics show this won't be the case, and what a rude awakening that will be.

Fortunately, comics are catching up with society. Readily available at the news stand are adventure series featuring nonwhite characters championing over evildoers. Not only are these tales exciting, but they send a subtle message that the forces of good in the universe come in all colors. DC Comics has recently issued adventures featuring male and female African American, Asian, and Latino superheroes to complement its line of Superman, Batman, and other costumed defenders of civilization.

And keep an eye and ear out for James Scott, an action figure employed by the twenty-first-century Planetary Law Enforcement Agency, dedicated to keeping the peace. First introduced on a non-profit radio station in 1984, this African American space hero's adventures are available in book and audio formats. It's interesting to note that the creator of the hero, Mike Sargent, first began drawing the character at age twelve.

Many parents carefully restrict moviegoing. The typical motivation is concern over sex or violence. You don't want Freddie Kruger in your child's dreams, and some movies contain intimate scenes that are obviously inappropriate for youngsters.

There is less care taken with in-home video viewing. Parents believe they can better supervise what is seen because they choose the video, and buttons on a remote control allow parents to pause or fast-forward through scenes that should not be seen.

But in addition to sex and violence, do you keep a careful eye on racial stereotypes? Perhaps they are considered less damaging. It's okay for a character to be bad, as long as he or she doesn't hurt or climb into bed with somebody.

Many adults today look back to movies that had a significant impact on their lives, and given that there are hundreds of motion pictures released every year (many of which make their way to video), it can be expected your children will feel the same way. America produces more movies than any other country. Since the dawn of this century, movies have been an extremely important component of our culture.

And also since then, movies have given short shrift to people of color or portrayed them as dangerous. That trend continues. As we mentioned earlier, there appears to be an openness to black filmmakers (not yet to Asians and Latinos, and recent efforts to portray Native Americans positively, such as *Dances With Wolves* and *Black Robe,* were directed by whites), but their films have not yet been embraced by a widespread audience. *Malcolm X,* the Spike Lee film released in late 1992, was an excellent vehicle for selling T-shirts and other souvenirs, but it didn't garner a cross section of viewers.

Let's consider the mainstream, popular films that more routinely wind up in your VCR. With few exceptions, such as the *Lethal Weapon* series and *Passenger 57,* videos do not contain nonwhite heroes. People of color are rarely cast as authority figures—police captains, government supervisors, lawyers and doctors, elected officials. Even the few times they are, they're peripheral characters not essential to the plot. And count how many times they are killed off!

One of the two most popular series of films in history is the *Star Wars* saga (the other being the *Indiana Jones* trilogy). Who is the dastardly villain? Darth Vader. Even if no connection is made to the implications of his first name, this character is dressed in black from head to toe. (His voice is supplied by the black actor James Earl Jones, though it's likely young children aren't aware of his color.) Luke Skywalker is a blond white youth, and his heroic colleagues fighting the evil empire that Vader represents are white, too.

Millions of youngsters have seen these films (and read the illustrated spin-off books). True, in the climactic scene of the first installment, it is revealed that under the sinister costume Vader is white, but does this one scene counteract the many other subtle associations that were made? (In the second installment, the character played by Billy Dee Williams, a black actor, betrays the hero and aligns himself with Vader's evil empire.)

Even animation has problems. *The Little Mermaid* is a fun movie, and the video is in millions of homes. Nonwhite viewers can reasonably be concerned with the portrayal of the character Sebastian, clearly played by a black man from the Caribbean, who is subservient to a white man and his teenage daughter.

While some adults dismiss this concern as picky, children are being given a subtle message. And again, how often do we see Latino, Asian, or other nonwhite characters in animated films? While Disney can be applauded for the darker skin tones of the characters in its megahit *Aladdin,* doesn't the portrayal of Indians in the earlier *Peter Pan* make you uncomfortable? Stereotypes persist, and they do influence children open to impressions.

One other area to discuss is advertising. Only a small percentage of commercials and print ads contain people of color or show diverse groups interacting. And it's interesting to note the controversy surrounding the advertising campaign for Benetton, the clothing chain, which prominently displays children of various races playing, hugging, and in other ways expressing affection for each other. Critics charge these ads are too bold or give a false impression of society. However, so do ads that exclude people of color.

Because of the heightened sensitivity of advertisers, TV and print campaigns don't rely on blatant stereotypes. The problem here is omission. To sell products, advertisements present an idealized environment where everyone is healthy, wealthy, and wise. With the exception of ads featuring famous athletes or that promote liquor (which, in a way, convey a stereotype), people of color are routinely omitted from this environment.

One example is a commercial for a national weekly business magazine that was shown repeatedly in 1992. First the editor in chief (middle-aged white male) speaks directly to the audience, then he leads it on a tour of the publication's departments to show viewers how hard his staff is laboring to gather intriguing, up-to-the-minute information. All of the editors and staff reporters are white. The few people of color shown are in the mailroom or clearly have clerical positions. Was this intentional? Probably not. Most likely, the ad reflects the racial composition of the publication. But still, the subtle implication is that people of color don't hold decision-making positions in important enterprises.

Another area is the selling of cosmetics and other personal products. The popular image of beauty is a young, white female, and of handsomeness, the young, white male. Though this advertising is directed at adults, children can't escape it—the ads are on TV, on mass-transportation placards, and on huge billboards. They portray an "ideal," giving white youngsters something to strive for while disenfranchising children of color as well as fostering a sense of invisibility, of unimportance, and perhaps of being less desirable.

And keep in mind there has been an intense effort among advertisers to produce commercials for children's shows, especially those on Saturday mornings to accompany cartoons. With few exceptions, youngsters are seeing white dolls, white characters eating candy bars and cereals, and white children riding skateboards and modeling clothes.

We know of a black couple who recently were at the home of white friends on a Saturday morning. A TV show was interrupted by a series of commercials pushing numerous products. The black couple's daughter asked, "How come they never show a black doll?" The expressions on the faces of the two white children sitting with her indicated this thought had never occurred to them. In a subtle way, these youngsters were learning that white dolls were the norm and a nonwhite doll would be an aberration, equating it with something strange, unattractive, and unimportant. Our own daughter, Dotteanna, asked, "Why don't they show black dolls, and when they do, why is the white doll always in the front?"

Rather startling was a commercial for Rappin' Barbie. Though the doll comes in both black and white versions, the one shown throughout the commercial is white. One version of the commercial shows a group of little girls (one is black, the others white) discussing what kind of Barbie they wanted for Christmas. Though several black Barbies are available, the doll the black girl said she wanted was white.

Children pick up on these images. Recently, Brendan, the son of one of the authors, had two friends over to play. Both friends were four-year-old girls, one white, the other black. The white girl had brought over her Ken and Barbie set, and she and Brendan began playing. Not wanting the black girl to feel left out of playtime, Brendan's mother found a Barbie (alas, relegated to the back of the closet) belonging to his eight-year-old sister. But the girl took one look at the white doll, tossed it aside, and asked for Legos. When the mother asked, "Can't she be friends with the other dolls?" the little girl replied, "Sure, but I want *my* doll to be friends with them, the one who looks like me."

Advertising on packaging has an effect too. One very popular break-fast cereal, Raisin Bran, in the summer of 1992 had its cover devoted to the Olympic basketball team. While we applaud the patriotic intent, the cover gave us pause: Of the twelve players on the team, only four were white, yet the box showed three white players and two black players, and both players standing in the front row were white. Too subtle? Not to children who gaze at the box every day as they eat breakfast and perhaps dream of future Olympic glory.

The objective of advertising is to offer the best possible world. But by avoiding people of color, it is presenting an unrealistic world, not the one your children will face in the twenty-first century, and not the one that is the best.

In our practice we often work with children who have felt the effects of racial stereotyping. One was an Asian child who kept stretching her eyes because what she had seen in the media impressed upon her that pretty girls had round eyes. Her self-worth was chal-lenged by a biased image of beauty.

Another case involved a Native American child who had been adopted by a white family. Amazingly, this youngster was afraid of Indians! Movies had given him the impression that Native Americans were violent and not to be trusted.

And there are white children who assume peers of color don't belong in certain scenarios. Betty is a fourth-grader interested in theater. Her elementary school was producing a version of the Beauty and the Beast fable. A black classmate wanted to play the prince, but Betty immediately objected, contending he was not right for the part. "You should be the Beast," she said. "He's dark, like you." When the teacher queried her about this assumption, Betty replied, "That's the way it is in my storybook and on the video!"

Especially at younger ages, children make visual associations. Col-ors make a profound impression. If your child is regularly presented with media that associates people of color with negative characteris-tics, it is no great leap to extend the resulting impressions to her real-world surroundings. Not only does this cause pain to peers of other racial backgrounds, but it gives her a mind-set that will impair her ability to coexist with others objectively as she approaches adolescence, and beyond. A superficial or false sense of superiority develops when self-esteem is desperately tied to being above all others at any cost, even at the risk of distorting or denying reality.

What can you do? Obviously, you cannot directly control the media unless you are a TV producer or magazine publisher or head an advertising agency, and there are dangerous implications to the concept of control of the media. For better and for worse, our media is an integral part of a democratic society.

But you can determine, to some extent, what the media presents and the impact it has on your child. Here are some recommendations:

• Monitor what your youngsters watch on TV (especially videos). If your circumstances require a baby-sitter, consider this: Do you give your baby-sitter free rein? You decide what your children can and cannot watch. If you think some programming is objectionable, make it off-limits. Though it takes some searching, there is enough variety on TV that your child won't be deprived of entertainment or enrichment.

• Instead of only mandating what can't be viewed, get involved in selecting appropriate alternatives. There are many programs on the Public Broadcasting System—especially "Sesame Street," "Reading Rainbow," "Ghostwriter," and "Mr. Rogers' Neighborhood"—that actively promote cultural diversity. A cable network like Nickelodeon also has multicultural programming. Encourage your children to watch the programs they carry. They are uplifting and a lot of fun.

• Inquire what videos your school shows. In many schools it is a common practice to show videos at midday when outdoor recess is canceled due to inclement weather. This is in addition to videos that may be shown in connection with the curriculum.

• When you watch TV with your child, discuss the images you see. In some cases, you will be trying to overcome a negative image, such as a news report or TV show that portrays people of certain races as uniformly violent or unsavory. Emphasize to him that this presents a view that is not true of an entire category of people.

In other cases, make the attempt to encourage positive views of other races. One example: When you see a character of another race, say, "Isn't he (she) attractive (smart, resourceful)?" With your approval, your child will be more inclined to empathize with or admire the character. Also point out similarities as well as differences between people of other races. For example, Louis, the son of close friends, loves the cartoon show "Ghostbusters." When he watches it, although he is white, he identifies with Winston, the only black man, "because Egon has yellow hair and Peter wears glasses but Winston is more like me."

Also encourage your child to discuss with you what she finds disturbing about a character, show, or advertisement. A stereotype could be one factor, and if your child feels open to talking about what bothers her, you can intervene before an unwholesome impression is made.

• If you disagree with a program or a station's programming in general, or the content of a publication, take ten minutes to write a letter of protest. Editors and producers are sensitive to public reaction, one reason being they don't receive enough of it.

Letters to the editor can be extremely effective. The same is true of TV stations. Every five years they have to apply for a renewal of their licenses to the Federal Communications Commission, which takes into account reaction from the community and is mandated by law to ensure racial and ethnic diversity in programming. You do have a say in what gets broadcast, especially on news shows.

One example we offer is that during the 1988 Olympics, some viewers were unhappy with the commentary on the figure skating competition between Debi Thomas of the United States and Katarina Witt of East Germany, because they thought it stereotyped the skaters' racial differences by repeatedly describing Thomas's performance as being athletic and forceful and Witt's as portraying beauty, grace, and skill. Many viewers called and wrote the network to complain. Subsequently, the network required that commentators upgrade their standards of reporting and focus on the abilities of competitors rather than perpetuating racial stereotypes. This change was evident in the coverage (by the same network) of the events in the 1992 Olympics.

• Write to advertisers for two reasons: (a) to inquire why their products' packaging does not reflect society's racial diversity and (b) to protest their sponsorship of TV programs that offer inaccurate or demeaning portraits of *any* racial group. A show that provides white characters who are objects of ridicule, uncool, or villainous in an interracial setting is not helpful to children of color.

• Every community has a local newspaper, and even major newspapers are vulnerable to criticism. All offer (though space varies) an op-ed page to which readers can submit opinion pieces and personal essays. If you think your newspaper has ignored or slighted a racial group, let the editors know. The smaller the circulation, the more effective your criticism—and the more likely your opinion will have an effect.

One simple, subtle example: Newspapers often publish photographs portraying the advent of spring or any day during the year when it is especially enjoyable to be outdoors. Look carefully and you'll see it's rare that a person of color is shown pushing his or her child on a swing. This omission reinforces the stereotype that people of color don't have stable families. Why, if you're a white parent, should you object? Because the repeated omission of people of color from these pleasant scenes will influence your child to accept the stereotype that only whites have stable families.

And when you do see a photo of a family of color enjoying a spring activity, point it out to your youngster, not in racial terms, but just showing the fun of a mild day.

• Do you watch talk shows? Obviously, some hosts, like Oprah Winfrey, Arsenio Hall, Montell Williams, and Geraldo Rivera, have attracted a wide audience, but more of these shows have white hosts, and their various topics are discussed on camera with predominately white guests. With very few exceptions, they simply do not deal with urgent issues that affect the Latino, Asian, and African American segments of the population.

Because these shows exist by popular appeal, contacting the producers will have an impact. Insist that they deal with issues relevant to your community and include more people of color. What relevance does this have to your child? Some preadolescents watch these shows (especially if the parent is not present!). Moreover, you need to consider the influence on yourself, which in turn has an impact on the signals about other races you send to your youngster.

• It's hard to criticize books, because they comprise such an important component of civilization. But the fact is that you have to be selective. How, in the words, are good and bad characters presented? How, in illustrations, are these characters presented?

Here's an exercise to try: Read a classic fairy tale without any references to color. Is it the same? Does it still convey the same moral lesson? If not, don't read it to your child. The tale might seem harmless to you, but you are not as innocent and impressionable as your child. Your comforting, loving bedside manner is planting a seed that will eventually separate colors into good and bad.

Even the most cursory search will result in your finding books at your library or local bookstore that offer characters of various colors and different settings. One author we highly recommend is Ezra Jack Keats. His stories are very enjoyable for children and portray youngsters of diverse backgrounds facing common situations. He's not the only one: Amy Tan, a well-respected author of adult fiction, also writes books for the children's market. (The Resource Guide lists other options.)

Recently one of the authors was in a bookstore in a predominantly white suburban community and found a large section of children's books devoted to stories about other cultures. This reinforces the belief that it takes little or no effort to find suitable books.

Be active, if necessary. Do you pay school taxes? That often means you have a say in what your local library carries, and certainly what your school library offers. Make an appointment with your librarian to discuss the books that are available or will be purchased for your child.

• Inevitably, due to economic forces, there will be more advertising directed at people of color. One area is TV. While the overall audience figures for the TV networks have declined, black households—accounting for 12 percent of the national pie—have assumed major importance. Advertisers will respond to this, and it gives viewers interested in multiracial programming more clout.

In general, to continue to be a force, advertising must reflect changing demographics. For Latinos, who are growing at 6.5 times the rate of the American population, the overall buying power is $180 billion, up from $100 million ten years ago. The Asian population in the United States more than doubled in the 1980s—the greatest increase of any ethnic group; numbering 7.5 million, Asian Americans have a buying power estimated at $110 billion. Again, manufacturers, publishers, and programmers will be responding to these markets.

One example of buying power advertisers need to heed? In January

1992, the U.S. Postal Service issued a "Happy New Year" stamp commemorating the Year of the Rooster. In San Francisco alone, two hundred thousand stamps were sold on the first day of issue. This became one of the ten top-selling stamps for first-day issue in a single city.

Advertisers must be held accountable for ignoring the dawning multicultural society. In August 1992, the New York City Department of Consumer Affairs released a study called "Still Invisible" that surveyed 2,108 ads in ten major nationally distributed publications, including magazines from *Better Homes and Gardens* to *Vogue*. The study found that blacks were featured in only 3.4 percent of magazine ads and 4.6 percent of mail-order catalogs. The department commissioner, Mark Green, wrote letters to the fourteen companies singled out as having the fewest minorities in their ads. Among them were Calvin Klein (0 out of 156 ads), Estée Lauder (0 out of 114), Cover Girl (1 out of 226), and Ralph Lauren (4 out of 138). (In September 1992, the Ralph Lauren Company did unveil a new advertising campaign featuring models of various colors.)

On the plus side, it would help to take a few moments each day and demonstrate to your child an appreciation of any advertising that features other racial groups. Be prepared to respond yourself to the expected increase in multiracial images.

We mentioned earlier in this chapter that the influence of the media can contradict your efforts to foster an appreciation of other cultures. We hope now you realize what that influence can be and that it doesn't have to be so pervasive.

The media exists because it seeks to fulfill what *we* want to see, hear, and read. The ardent supporters of media claim it can provide its audience with a progressive path to follow by offering new and interesting information or entertainment that improves our lives. We agree. That's why it is so important that the media embrace—on every page, program, and advertisement—the reality of the multicultural society that all of our children will participate in.

Part III

A Positive Approach

8
Social Studies

Tod Moran grew up in a suburban community that developed rapidly in the late 1950s and early 1960s. Families moved out from the city seeking a better life that included owning their homes, sending their children to new and uncrowded schools, being surrounded by relatively open space, and escaping the fear of urban crime. Tod was unaware at the time of another, understated reason: Some white families wanted to leave neighborhoods whose racial composition was changing.

There were few black students at Tod's school, and no Latinos or Asians. He didn't notice this lack of racial diversity, he simply accepted that this was what a "normal" suburban community was like. An adjacent community was comprised of mostly black families, with some Latinos, yet there were no functions or events at which members of the two communities interacted. Because his parents rarely mentioned people of color, Tod did not have a positive or negative view of them.

One day, when Tod was nine, he was playing basketball with several friends when three black youngsters arrived at the school yard. All the boys joined in a long game that left them happily tired. Play had been furious yet fair, and the teams so evenly matched it didn't really matter which won.

As the black youngsters were leaving, Tod shouted to them to come by again the next day. Yet as soon as they were out of earshot Ben, one of Tod's friends, said, "Don't tell 'em something like that. They'll bring all their friends."

"So what?" Tod responded. "We had a great game. They seemed like nice guys."

Ben laughed at him. "I better straighten you out. Don't you know there are good blacks and there are niggers? Who knows what's going to show up next time."

Not long after this, Tod's aunt and uncle came over for a visit. Their son, Larry, was sixteen and had just gotten his driver's license. He was asked to go to a store for ice and soda, and Tod accompanied him.

Being unfamiliar with the roads, Larry drove past the turnoff for the shopping center and in a few minutes entered the other community. Tod saw how nervous his cousin became, and he assured Larry he knew the way back.

"Yeah, but we just gotta live long enough to get there," Larry muttered, his hands gripping the steering wheel. "Well, they won't get us without a fight."

"W-who?" Tod stammered. "What fight?"

Larry reached under his seat and brought out a small bat. "I got the enforcer here," the teen said. "Any of the natives try anything, this'll turn 'em into jelly."

As Tod grew up and was exposed to other racial groups, especially at college, he looked back at these and other incidents with revulsion. He married, he and his wife had two children, and the suburban neighborhood they moved to in the 1980s was racially mixed. He and his wife made sure to say positive things about other races in front of their children, they forbade adult relatives from negatively influencing their children, they carefully monitored TV shows and other media exposure, and they attended school events at which all races and their cultures were represented. Tod was pleased that the cycle of unreasonable fear and hatred had been broken.

Or so he thought. One afternoon his son, Terry, seven, returned from a hike his after-school program had gone on. Instead of saying it was fun, Terry expressed relief that it was over. When Tod asked what had gone wrong, the boy replied, "We had some black kids with us, and I sure didn't want to be out in the woods with them."

"Why not?" Tod inquired.

"I didn't know what they might do," Terry said. "Ronnie at school, he told me when blacks get out in the woods, it reminds them of the jungle and they think about eating people."

Tod was devastated. How could people still be saying such awful things? And given the attitude of Tod and his wife, how could their son possibly consider such a preposterous story as the truth?

. . .

This anecdote illustrates a situation that a good number of well-meaning parents have to confront—the power of peers to impress prejudice on their children. As they spend more time outside the home and friends become more of a factor in their lives, even the most open-minded and secure youngsters can be influenced by peers who for various reasons are not prepared for a multicultural society.

This is not to say peer groups themselves are a problem. Having an expanding circle of acquaintances and several close friends is essential to healthy development. Children who are loners or who have difficulty interacting with peers can develop interpersonal problems that affect the rest of their lives.

Peer groups offer a setting of comfort, support, and much positive stimulation. Children are emotionally enriched by having friends they can turn to to share happiness or to be consoled. Parents often feel they would like to be all things to their children and can fulfill every need. The bittersweet fact is that there is only so much we can provide, and as they get older we gradually have to let our kids go out into the world and hope we've given them a solid foundation so they can weather any storm.

Many of the experiences youngsters have with peers are good ones. Our children learn about sharing, they empathize with others, they see how other families live, they discover mutual interests, they are physically and intellectually active in a variety of games, information is given and received, and in general friends are fun. We might not like all the friends our children make—one boy whines, one girl seems rude, another has a habit of breaking things, and another is too boastful about athletic prowess—yet we realize it's in their best interests developmentally to be part of the gang.

The downside is, there are negative influences, too, and they can be potent. When a well-behaved child starts to talk back in an impolite manner, it could be due to hearing a friend talk disrespectfully to an adult. We ache when our son or daughter cries because a friend has chosen to play with someone else or they've had a fight. With somewhat older children, we could be concerned that they're being exposed to such unwholesome activity as stealing, vulgar language, or substance abuse.

Another negative influence is prejudice. No matter how much effort you've put into promoting respect for others, inevitably your youngster will be confronted with peers whose parents don't feel the way you do or haven't made a similar effort. Children who fear other racial groups feel better if their friends are "on our side." Because of the strong emotional ties between friends and the fragile self-esteem of youngsters, it is very difficult to withstand peer pressure.

Timothy is a middle-school student involved in many activities, from sports to the science club. His parents are happy that he seems so well-adjusted and fond of school. But they begin to notice that he is especially tired after school. At dinner he can't eat enough, yet if anything he appears to have lost some weight. After several weeks they sit him down for a talk. After some hesitation, Timothy reveals the problem: He doesn't eat lunch anymore.

At school, the students in the cafeteria group themselves by race. White students sit in one section, blacks in another, and Asians and Latinos have their own enclaves. While Timothy enjoys sitting with his black peers, he has friends among the other groups, and he likes to spend time with them, too. Increasingly, however, his black peers have accused him of preferring other races.

"You're ashamed of being black," they charged.

"Get out," Timothy responded indignantly. "I'm proud of my color."

"Which color?" they taunted. "What do you really want to be— white? yellow? *Habla español?*"

Though he resented these comments, Timothy decided to stay with his own group. But this caused another problem. A source of amusement in the group was to ridicule students in the other groups and make condescending or really hurtful remarks. Timothy was uncomfortable with this and felt worse when his peers ridiculed him for not being "bold" enough. Eventually, he avoided the cafeteria entirely.

At his parents' urging, Timothy spoke to a couple of black peers he thought he could trust and found that they shared the same concerns but were uncomfortable about taking the initiative to create change. They decided to work together in beginning to integrate the cafeteria. They realized there would always be some students who would refuse to eat with peers of another color, but they believed the example of several students making an effort would attract attention and a positive response.

The age of your child determines the level of concern for peer-pressure prejudice. While preschool children are capable of ganging up on a friend, rarely is racism a factor. These youngsters are still forming judgments about peers visibly different from themselves, and any mention of racial differences is usually caused by curiosity.

Brendan, the four-year-old son of one of the authors, plays with Adam, a boy of the same age, every summer when Adam is staying with his grandmother up the street. Last summer, as the boys were taking a break from playing with model race cars, Brendan reached out his hand and touched the tightly curled black hair on Adam's head. Smiling, and feeling his own straight blond hair, Brendan said, "I like your hairdo. How did you get that?" Adam shrugged and replied, "That's my hair. It's always there." The boys returned to their model cars.

School-age children are more likely to form alliances to exclude someone they fear, mistrust, or dislike—and sometimes for what appears to be no reason at all, just a whim. As children grow older and become more emotionally entangled, peer groups represent as much or more of a need fulfillment than the home environment. For youngsters with unpleasant home environments (due to death, divorce, substance or other abuse, extreme poverty), the peer group represents a source of support or shelter.

Unfortunately, one way peer group members feel more bonded together is by targeting another group or individual for scorn and ridicule. Prejudice is a motivating factor if some or all members of the group have been negatively influenced by parents, relatives, teachers, or the media. Though a group member might have been raised with respect for other races, he might go along with the gang mentality rather than risk ridicule or ostracism.

If your child is spending more time with friends than family, that doesn't mean you have lost control of teaching racial appreciation. But it does mean you have competition in steering her in the right direction. If, like Tod Moran in the opening anecdote, you realize misinformation or peer pressure jeopardizes your appreciation efforts, here are several suggestions:

• Spend time with your child's friends and try to influence them positively in creating acceptance and respect for others.
• Involve your child in a peer group that fosters acceptance and appreciation of differences. Among the possibilities are a church group, an after-school program, a Cub or Brownie pack, or ad hoc gatherings held specifically to explore racial diversity.
• Establish relationships with people in surrounding communities if you live in an exclusively single-race community. Look for activities in those communities in which to participate.
• Immediately challenge remarks of peers reported to you by your child or uttered in your presence. Point out what is not only hurtful but inaccurate. You might have accurate information to offer at the moment, or invite your child and his or her peers to join you on an outing to the library or a museum where positive and accurate information about the maligned racial group is available.

More so than younger children, school-age children model their behavior and form racial attitudes by observing the actions of their parents. Earlier in this book we discussed the influence of subtle signals. Now we want to discuss obvious actions, such as how adults interact with their own peers.

It is not uncommon for people to enter adulthood without ever having visited the home of a different race. And though in high school or college you sat in multiracial classrooms and belonged to multiracial clubs, how integrated were social settings? When your parents hosted a barbecue or holiday gathering, how many (if any!) guests were members of other races? How often were you invited to other groups' parties?

Now, as adults, look back and count how many times you have socialized with other races and ask yourself how long were the intervals between those experiences. As the cliche goes, action speaks louder than words, so your children are filing away the fact that you rarely, if at all, are involved in multiracial socializing.

Judy Frisson is a CPA and the mother of two children. Both she and her husband, Ed, a mail carrier, work alongside Latinos, Asians, and African Americans. They enjoy each other's company at work, occasionally go out to lunch, and give each other gifts at holidays and birthdays. When the Frissons think of friends, included in that category are several people from the workplace.

Yet they have never invited Latino, Asian, or African American co-workers to their home for dinner or parties. Judy and Ed rationalize that, away from work, they want to unwind, which they couldn't really do with co-workers because so much of the conversation would be "shop talk." Still, when they invite neighbors over, they too are all white, though they are friendly with nonwhite families. They think people of color would be uncomfortable in their home, just as they would probably be uncomfortable in theirs.

Judy and Ed send their children to a multiracial school, they are careful not to utter racial slurs or condescending remarks, and from time to time when having dinner each praises a co-worker, making sure to point out the person's race. They seem to have covered the bases, and they believe it really would be going too far to drag people to their home who likely don't want to be invited in the first place.

While Judy and Ed's thinking is all too common, there are many examples of co-workers of different races establishing stronger ties. For example, when one of the authors recently had a baby shower, co-workers, friends, and family attended. As gifts were being opened, it was pleasing to survey the room and see parents and children of various racial backgrounds talking, playing, and sitting together. Not only was it a heartening scene to the author, but the children in the room at some level were aware of their parents and parents' friends interacting and having a good time.

Despite changing demographics in the United States, many communities remain racially segregated. Even in urban areas, entire blocks can be inhabited by one racial group, and on multiracial blocks there can be buildings that house only same-race dwellers. While we might bump into people of other races, we often don't interact socially. And it's not uncommon that in some affluent, predominantly white neighborhoods, the only people of color to be seen are maids, nannies, and yard workers who leave at the end of the day.

Children are aware of the social segregation of their parents. It's not that they are necessarily disturbed by this; it's more likely they gradually accept that people should "stay with their own kind." But there are several risks to this attitude.

One is that eventually most youngsters will find themselves in multiracial settings, such as community organizations, schools, or college campuses, without having had an opportunity to model behavior from observing their parents. They can feel awkward, mistrustful, or even afraid. Certainly the increase in bias incidents on campuses across the country indicates that many teenagers and young adults of diverse backgrounds simply don't know how to live together.

The other risk is that (because demographics are changing so dramatically) many communities will no longer retain the racial composition that might have been present for decades. Before your children enter adolescence, your community will become multiracial. And with fewer and fewer exceptions, the communities your children live in as adults will be racially diverse. The social segregation of today will make it more difficult for the next generation to live comfortably side by side.

A third risk is that without exposure to other races, misperceptions will prevail. "Two Neighborhoods, Two Worlds," by Isabel Wilkerson, is an article published in the June 21, 1992, issue of the *New York Times* that examined the Roseland and Mount Greenwood communities in northern Illinois. The former was all black, the latter all white. One Mount Greenwood resident was quoted as saying that it infuriates her that "blacks buy porterhouse steaks with food stamps while we eat hamburgers." However, she had never actually seen blacks do this but "has heard and read stories, and that is enough." Other white residents said they worked alongside blacks from Roseland and that they were "lovely people," yet they were fearful of blacks in general because they didn't know what they were like away from work.

We have conducted Positive Play workshops in several major cities across the country, including Chicago and Los Angeles. In each geographical area the children were highly responsive, but there were also some very interesting differences observed given the varying regions and settings.

For example, children from a segregated, inner-city section in Chicago, when asked the question, "Can Shani [African American fashion doll] be friends or play with Barbie?" most of the children responded, "No!" Children from a highly integrated section of Los Angeles responded to the same question with a resounding, "Yes!" Several of these children further explained, "It did not matter if they were black or white, but how they felt about each other."

It was quite clear, once again, how early experiences within segregated or integrated settings can prohibit or foster the ability to form healthy acceptance and appreciation of differences.

What can you do? One action is to go ahead and take the plunge by inviting a black, white, Latino, or Asian friend to your home. What will the neighbors think? Well, you can't expect your child to adequately deal with peer pressure if you allow that same pressure to influence your decisions. And if you are invited to another's home, think before you offer an excuse: Is it really due to racial differences?

Perhaps you think a dinner or party invitation is too formal. Another action to consider is, if your child plays with a friend of another race, to invite the parent (or yourself!) over for coffee. For example, when Donna's mother stops by to pick up her daughter, ask her in for a few minutes to chat. It is likely you will find many common topics to discuss, and both children will be observing the rapport you establish.

In every city and in most communities there are events (parades, bake sales, sports, concerts, picnics, block parties) that attract a multiracial and multigenerational audience. Attend them with your family. These are usually very comfortable settings for people to socialize across racial lines. You will observe the children happily cavorting with each other, and even if it's unconsciously, the children will be aware that the grown-ups are enjoying each other's company.

In July 1992, one of the authors invited his mother to a neighborhood block party. Of the two hundred people at the party, ranging in age from infants to elderly people, nearly three-quarters were African American and Latino. The author's mother, who had been raised and then lived in white communities, was clearly uncomfortable for the first hour. She looked as though she had suddenly found herself on another planet and didn't know how to communicate with the aliens.

But she found herself drawn to an adjacent table where four black women of similar age were exchanging photos and stories about their grandchildren. Sometime later, when the author next looked over, his mother had shifted her chair to the table and, with one of her grandchildren on her knee, was offering her own anecdotes.

When the party ended, this group was one of the last to leave. "What nice people," the author's mother commented, her expression implying that she and the other women had more in common than she ever thought possible. There is little doubt that the hour or so spent with the other women made an impression on the grandchild who stayed with her.

Adults are funny folks. Though they are considered mature, they can feel that "I won't socialize with so-and-so because he (she) probably doesn't want me to," and there is a lifelong fear of rejection. Go ahead, give it a try. If you have become friendly with someone of another color through a school organization or work, extend a social invitation. A cup of coffee or a poker game is not too much of an emotional investment.

You might be rebuffed, but try again with someone else. If you feel awkward, keep in mind that a big reason for making the overture is your child. And who knows? Like the author's mother, you might really enjoy the get-together. If you belong to a church or temple, there is another option. Every day, there are examples across the country of churches inviting members of nearby congregations of a different color to join in services or activities. A common and powerful link between the groups is their worship, which can lay a strong foundation that makes color differences insignificant. Build upon this foundation by organizing religious and social events that bring adults and children together.

Let's backtrack a bit to the peer pressure your youngster could experience. As we've stressed in this book, and as is the case with most things in life, prevention is priceless. With peer pressure, preparing your child to resist or combat prejudice is the best way to help guide him through situations outside the home that you can't control.

What does this preparation consist of? Again, we emphasize: It must begin early, before your youngster begins full-time schooling. It is a tremendous advantage if you encourage an appreciation of other cultures, monitor the media, and contradict adults who bring negative attitudes into your home. But to some extent, this is a reactive strategy. You are a fire fighter ready to put out any blaze that should start up.

We urge you to be proactive. Get involved in exposing your child to multiracial peers. Children love to play with other children, and after years of routine exposure, the ridicule or fear of other races, not the other races themselves, will seem strange and unsavory.

We have several recommendations on how to get started:

• Participate in (or organize) a multiracial play group. Local churches, libraries, and some schools provide neutral settings. As the toddlers interact, they accept as natural brown, black, white, and yellow grown-ups standing or sitting together.

• Do you rely on day care? Many parents do while they're at work, or they believe it's a good peer experience. Choose a program that has children of diverse racial backgrounds. Without parents present, children are more apt to form an emotional attachment and dependence on each other that has nothing to do with what color they are.

• At a play group or day-care center, and in your own home, make sure that dolls, toys, and games reflect racial diversity. From the age of two on, children do symbolic play; they begin to use their imaginations and use playthings to act out daily life experiences.

• Every child enjoys a playground, whether it's at a school or the local park. In most communities, urban and suburban, playgrounds attract children of every color. Beware of any impulse to steer your child toward groups of children with the same racial background as yours. That sends a message. Just let your child play. And make the effort to spend a few minutes with every group of parents standing or sitting on the sidelines. Just as you are keeping a watchful eye on your child, she is regularly making sure of where you are and what you are doing.

• When you are choosing a nursery school, do you consider the racial composition? The two or three mornings or afternoons a week children spend with their peers in nursery school provide an excellent opportunity to interact with and appreciate peers different from themselves. They learn and play together and begin to discover that barriers to friendship have nothing to do with color.

• From nursery school on, there is a wide variety of after-school programs and activities—arts and crafts, holiday costume making, music, story hours. These are often in multiracial settings, and you can get involved to ensure that activities represent a variety of cultures.

• Be alert for community events and organizations that attract a diverse audience. The local 4-H club and Cub Scout or Brownie pack help teach children about nature and mutual cooperation. This is a wonderful opportunity for children to discover (or to reinforce from previous experiences) that being able to play and work together has little to do with skin color.

• If you relocate, look for a multiracial community to move into. By purposely isolating yourself in a same-color neighborhood, you create a wall that will be difficult for your child to scale as he approaches adolescence.

We don't mean to imply that if your child is well into the school-age years and some of the above preparation hasn't been done, it's too late to overcome peer pressure. Yes, the obstacles are more formidable. There is the possibility that whatever you show or say is being contradicted to some extent by what she is seeing or hearing among friends.

First, we want to stress the belief that there are more parents like you out there, people who also realize their children must be prepared for the multicultural society of the twenty-first century. We think this means that many of the friends your child makes will not be negative influences but will also have an appreciation of others, and we will see more multiracial peer groups.

Second, however strong the pressure of peers, your child will ultimately seek your support and approval. If something is bothering your son or daughter, he or she wants to discuss it with you. On a regular basis—in addition to when your child seeks your counsel—instigate discussions about dilemmas created by peer pressure. While the situation of a child growing older inspires some misgivings and poignant thoughts, this stage also provides opportunities for more interactive, sophisticated conversations. You will understand each other better. And he or she will walk away from a discussion appreciating the fact that you have respected his or her feelings and the hurdles to be overcome.

Third, there are times when peer pressure can be extremely positive and rewarding. We close with an anecdote that certainly inspired us:

A troop of Boy Scouts planned to camp out in a wooded setting, which happened to be on the grounds of a private club. Permission was sought and granted for the weekend trip. The troop, which included white and black youngsters, was excited as they packed up their gear.

But when they arrived at the entrance to the grounds, club officials there noticed the racial composition of the group and proclaimed that the black scouts could not participate in the campout. A private club had the right to refuse blacks.

The boys conferred among themselves and decided that if they could not all participate, then none of them would. The troop leaders drove them to a public campground, where they spent the weekend. We can only imagine the feelings these boys shared when peer pressure resulted in a one-for-all, all-for-one attitude—a sense of respect and empathy for one another.

We do believe that this shared experience will likely last them a lifetime.

9

Spreading the Good Word . . . and Image

In a previous chapter we discussed the views of people who live in adjacent communities near Chicago: Many black and white residents saw each other in certain ways that relied on stereotypes. In these communities, as in many others with residents of diverse racial backgrounds, stereotypes persist because people simply don't know enough about each other. They don't think there's anything wrong with their attitudes and have no intention of changing them.

By reaching this point in the book, you are poised to walk through a door. It leads to a twenty-first-century multicultural American society that has an appreciation of all its various components and colors. This door represents an exciting opportunity to prepare your children, and in the process you might reevaluate your own views. The goal here is to learn more about other people.

We have stressed the necessity to teach youngsters how to appreciate different people and cultures. Some of you might think the term "teach" implies a chore, a spoonful of unpleasant medicine that must be swallowed. Especially if you don't have fond memories of your own educational experience, you might hesitate to embark with your child on this learning journey.

But if you've spent any time recently in an elementary classroom, chances are good you've noted that teaching today involves creativity, play, a wide range of stimulating learning tools, and a desire on the part of teachers to make learning a fun, interactive experience.

Similarly, teaching an appreciation of other cultures need not be a boring task. It can be one of the most enjoyable parts of your relationship with children. Yet the key is that you must be involved. Hand in hand, you and your child can take the first steps along the path and marvel at the many attractions surrounding you.

As with any place that is unfamiliar, you might have to act as a scout, surveying the terrain before signaling your child to follow. A comment we often hear from parents is, "I don't know that much about _____ people and their culture. How can I expect to teach my child?"

This is a reasonable and wise comment. Misinformation can be worse than no information at all. We applaud those parents who, rather than seem like know-it-alls or avoid talking about topics they're unsure about, admit they lack an adequate amount of information.

If you are one of those parents, now is the time for some adult education. No, we're not suggesting you enroll at a college or other educational institution—though if you have the time and money, by all means go for it. Just learn enough so that you'll be able to answer your child's questions or, if you're stumped by questions, you will have a pretty good idea of where to go for answers. Your child will sense your openness, curiosity, or confidence.

The easiest way is probably the most effective: the resources available at a nearby library. While books on racial and cultural differences have been written for decades, within the last few years publishers have been devoting an increasing amount of attention to these subjects. Ask your librarian for help in finding such books, as well as articles in various parenting magazines. Books not available at the local library can usually be requested from other libraries in the system, or a bookstore can order them from the publishers.

An even easier way to start is to look in the Resource Guide of this book. While we offer only a sampling, reading any one or two of the books will provide a solid foundation of information.

Get involved in what's going on at your child's school. Parents are sometimes surprised that their children seem to know more about cultural diversity than they do. Curricula have been broadened, and progressive teachers and administrators have been making special efforts to introduce youngsters to cultures around the world. They rely on certain materials and would be very happy to share them with you. Teachers often lament that they do not get enough input or notice enough curiosity from parents.

Many national organizations with chapters in your community, and local groups as well, have been paying more attention to cultural diversity, especially as their memberships have become more racially diverse. Even if your child is too young to participate in these organizations, its leaders have done some research and can share their findings with you or at least point you in the right directions. One example is a workshop called Developing Pluralistic Attitudes in Children, conducted by the Girl Scouts of America. In some communities, organizations exist for the sole purpose of forging links between racial groups.

Museums and other cultural institutions frequently offer exhibits devoted to other cultures. These exhibits are usually for grown-ups and children, but sometimes there is a show specifically designed to increase awareness among adults. An example is Ethnic Images in Toys and Games, which was held at the history museum of the State University of New York at Stony Brook in the fall of 1991. It traced how, for much of this century, some games, toys, and dolls were modeled on stereotypical images. No doubt parents came away from this exhibit with a better understanding of how young minds can be negatively influenced.

Another example is an exhibit called The Kids Bridge, held in early 1993 at the Smithsonian Institution in Washington, D.C. It was the first ever presented specifically for children at the Smithsonian, and it included a booth where visitors listened to lullabies in several languages; pushcarts displaying food, clothing, and toys from numerous cultures; a video display of children saying everyday phrases in native languages; hopscotch boards for the game as it is played in China, Ethiopia, and Italy; and a short video of children of diverse backgrounds talking about their perceptions of other children. At this writing the exhibit is in the midst of a three-year tour that will bring it to museums in Indianapolis; Miami; Houston; Chicago; Philadelphia; Bridgeport, Connecticut; Stockton, California; and Portland, Oregon.

Also in 1993 was an exhibit at the Balch Institute for Ethnic Studies in Philadelphia, Rites of Passage in America: Traditions of the Life Cycle, which contained photographs and artifacts that showed how Americans from eighteen different ethnic backgrounds celebrate life's important events. It's hard to think of a more congenial and inexpensive way to expose your child to other cultures.

Talk to people you are acquainted with who have different racial backgrounds—teachers, co-workers, neighbors, community leaders, owners of businesses you frequent. We realize this could cause some awkwardness, and you could approach someone who is particularly sensitive and might find your questions condescending. But we sincerely believe that in the vast majority of situations, the person you approach will appreciate your motive. Ask about her family's history, his cultural influences, whether parenting styles differ based on backgrounds, and share experiences that involved bigotry. One reason why prejudice persists is that many people never get to understand its effect on victims, especially innocent ones like children.

An active role you can take in your home is to designate certain evenings as cultural nights. Depending on your culinary skills, make dishes native to other countries (tempering some ingredients to the tolerance level of your family's taste buds!) and perhaps follow any rituals associated with that night's culture. Maybe these nights can coincide with holidays important to other cultures. If you can squeeze it in, prepare explanations for these rituals. Start off with a country that has always intrigued you.

A truly proactive approach is to form a discussion group of like-minded parents. This is very helpful if you and your peers have limited time; each member can bring a separate bit of information to the gathering to share. Gatherings can also include guest participants—people of different backgrounds who can share their culture, child-raising concerns, and views of the racial climate in the community.

Such a group can offer another benefit: conflict resolution. One reason why bias incidents can escalate to the point where they engulf entire neighborhoods or communities is that people don't talk to each other—there is no mechanism in place to handle tension. A group of well-intentioned parents, especially if comprised of people of all colors in the community, can address an incident, its causes and consequences, and seek solutions before tempers go beyond the point of reason.

There is one more advantage to any form of adult education on racial issues: Your child will know you care. He will see you reading a book and might express curiosity. She wants to know about the meeting you attended, and why. And as you feel more confident to discuss sensitive matters, your child will pick up on this and, through the years, will turn to you for answers instead of relying on less-informed sources.

. . .

When you're ready to go exploring with your child, we again urge you to take advantage of our Resource Guide. In it we list many tools you can use in your home—books, videos, dolls, games. Share them. It does help simply to make these sources available to your child, but a much deeper impression is made if together you read a book, watch a video, listen to a tape, or play a game.

Beyond what you do together, as a parent you can determine what materials your child uses by herself. For example, you might not look at a comic book together but you can buy a comic book you want your child to read. Traditionally, superheroes have been white males, but this is changing, as we discussed in the chapter on media.

The journey with your child involves more than reading and watching. The following anecdote shows how parents took advantage of opportunities to educate themselves and their child.

Pat and Mike Berson, a white couple in their mid-thirties, have a seven-year-old son and live in a predominantly white neighborhood. They are concerned that in the community and in school Hugh does not have enough exposure to people of other races and that without intervention he will not develop an appreciation of other cultures.

From the time Hugh was born they have decorated his room and portions of their home with pictures of figures from American history, thinking this was visually pleasing as well as educational. But after they learned more about cultural diversity and society's changing demographics, they decided to alter what was on the walls. In addition to pictures of Washington, Lincoln, the first moon landing, and other famous persons and scenes, they prominently displayed portraits of Martin Luther King, Jr., Thurgood Marshall, Sitting Bull, Nelson Mandela addressing the U.S. Congress, the 1991 Little League championship team from Taiwan, Roberto Clemente and Ruben Sierra (Hugh really liked baseball), Nancy Lopez lining up a winning putt at a tournament, Barbara Jordan speaking from her wheelchair to the 1992 Democratic convention, and others that showed people of diverse backgrounds who had contributed to American history or culture.

From time to time Hugh asked about one of the pictures, and either his parents gave him whatever information they knew or they went to the local library together. Even when he didn't ask, the Bersons believed that in a subtle way their son was becoming comfortable with the country's multicultural background.

One day, as Mike drives his son to his first Saturday of Little League practice, Hugh suddenly points and says, "What's that?" Mike observes that over the winter a new building has been erected, an Islamic mosque, no doubt to serve the Pakistani immigrants who have recently moved into the area. Mike explains that it is a house of worship, like their church, and suggests that after practice they stop by the library to take out some books on the Islamic religion. Later that afternoon, as a family they looked through some picture books showing mosques and the geography of Pakistan.

Especially with young children, words and images have a profound effect. So too the involvement of their parents in learning experiences. Not long ago we did a pilot study where we showed elementary school children pictures of a white man and a black man and asked the youngsters which type of person did they think had invented the roller coaster, the gas mask, the alarm clock, the baby crib, potato chips, or ice cream, or had discovered blood plasma. The majority of children, black and white, pointed to the picture of the white male, when in fact blacks were responsible. This is an example of the importance of raising awareness among youngsters of the contributions of all races to American history, science, and culture.

Use this time to bring into your home tools that reflect a changing society. The exposure you provide now will be a comfortable, supportive one, and questions can be immediately addressed. You are laying a foundation that will enable your youngster to reject, or at least objectively explore, the negative influences that are inevitable as he or she goes out into the world.

Time for a field trip? As important as the home environment is, and no matter how earnest your efforts to bring positive words and images into your home, there is a huge classroom outside your door. We urge you to help your child encounter and enjoy the diversity of that classroom.

Once again we mention museums, because children are often fascinated by exhibits that show other cultures and civilizations. It doesn't have to be all dinosaurs!

Exhibits on human evolution can be particularly instructive as well as entertaining. Some exhibits are based on the latest scientific findings, some of which—for example, DNA research currently under way—contend that all of humankind evolved from Africans. The object here is not to credit any one race but to show that in history's view racial differences are not all that great or even very important.

An article in the September 16, 1991, issue of *U.S News & World Report* on this latest research stated:

> *We will have to fundamentally change our view of who we are. [Research] suggests that in the end, all humans are in essence Africans and far more closely related than we might imagine. Indeed, gene research reveals that there is more genetic variability among the members of any one race than there is between different races. A Caucasian, for instance, might be genetically more similar to an Asian or African than to another Caucasian.*

Further research will determine if this contention is fact, but it at least presents us with the possibility that from the beginnings of human life we are more alike than different.

After considering such information, through an exhibit or reading, it would be more difficult for any youngster to develop the biased view that any one race is inferior to another. We are, in a sense, all branches of the same tree.

Take your child to a concert of one of the dozens of performers who specialize in children's music. Many of these performers have been leaders in incorporating into their repertoires the music of many countries, and often they will introduce a song with an appropriate folktale. If these performers don't get to your area or if ticket prices are prohibitive, buy a tape or borrow one from the library. Look in the Resource Guide for some suggestions.

Another outing option is to attend a lecture. Because multiculturalism is becoming a topic of wider popular appeal, it is easier to find in or near your community talks given by people who discuss racial differences. One example we can think of is Giancarlo Esposito, an actor who appeared in the film *Do the Right Thing* and who now makes over fifty appearances a year on college campuses and at other institutions with a program called Confronting Race in America. (While this and some other presentations might not be appropriate for children, they offer opportunities in multiracial settings for you to hear discussions on race relations and what people of other backgrounds think about multicultural issues.)

Some parents believe that sending their children to camp for a week or for the entire summer is an enriching experience. In recent years there has been a leap in the number of multicultural camps across the country. Children of various races live together for days or weeks and share their family histories and rituals, their concerns and hopes. Especially if the school your child attends is predominantly of one race, such a camp offers a good opportunity for him or her to learn about other people and to learn that having fun and depending on each other has nothing to do with skin color.

If programs do not already exist in your community, town, or city, consider forming a multiracial children's group to do projects together. More so than most adults, children seek creative outlets for their fears, discomfort, or just curiosity. Such a group, with parental guidance, should be encouraged to compose songs, produce plays, write their own folk or fairy tales, make paintings. Studies have shown that in group work youngsters are quick to form allegiances that ignore racial or ethnic differences (one reason why schools are increasingly employing this learning method). Every week a different parent can host the group and suggest subjects based on his or her own cultural background. In the process of having fun, the children will learn that anyone of any color can display talent, a spirit of cooperation, a need for help—and a high degree of just plain silliness!

Holidays present excellent opportunities to appreciate other cultures. With the exception of Martin Luther King, Jr.'s birthday, holidays devoted to people of color are not on the official calendar. But these days are easily found, and February is Black History Month. In your home, in your child's school, and among any group you've helped to form you can offer or participate in celebrations with accompanying racial or cultural background information.

An anecdote offers one example:

Columbus Day was approaching, and Donald, a ten-year-old, sat in class listening to a story about Christopher Columbus. The story included statements to the effect that the explorer had set out for the New World and that he had discovered America. But from history lessons and other stories his parents had read him, Donald was confused: How could Columbus discover a land where people—Indians—were already living and had a thriving culture? Weren't they called *Native Americans?*

After the story, Donald asked his teacher about this. Giving his question some thought, she agreed that "discover" was a poor word to use and did overlook Native Americans. Donald was encouraged to research and write his own story—which he did with his parents' input—that described life in America before the visit of Columbus, and he read it to the class.

(We'd like to add here that Dr. Ivan Van Sertima, a professor of African studies at Rutgers University, believes after twenty-two years of study that there is evidence that Africans were already present in America when Columbus arrived. This position casts more doubt on the Eurocentric view that the fifteenth-century explorer *discovered* America, as does ongoing research into longstanding claims that Chinese or Scandinavian mariners arrived at these shores.)

Something to keep in mind, however, is that these celebrations should not be considered the only time attention is paid to other cultures. A little research will provide a year-round awareness. We recall a teacher who, when Black History Month ended, removed from the classroom pictures of black people, replacing them with images of spring. Portraits of white historical figures were left on the walls.

This sent the clear message that an appreciation of black culture and history in America is a one-shot deal and, perhaps, a temporary aberration. And imagine the feelings of Latino, Asian, and Native American students who don't have any officially designated period devoted to their cultures. Throughout the year there are reasons to celebrate the contributions of other races and cultures, and by making the effort yourself or urging the school to give adequate attention to these contributions, you are emphasizing that we live in a society that wouldn't be the same without them.

We hope our suggestions don't seem painful. It doesn't help to think, "I really can't get into this, but I'll do it for my kids. And if they don't like it, too bad; I'll make them learn."

Children have a natural curiosity about people, places, and events.

Most don't care about the color of the person who did this or that, invented something, or inspired a generation. It's just interesting stuff. And if they learn it through play or cooperation among peers, so much the better. They had fun, and they learned something.

Of course, we all know from our own early experiences that one can learn things in boring, uninspired, or even punitive contexts. How many of us wanted to learn trigonometry? But most of us did (ugh!) because we had to in order to graduate from high school. And how much of it really stuck? Do you remember what "mitochondria" means from science class? or what role Claudio or Beatrice plays in Shakespeare's *Much Ado About Nothing?*

We want to stress (even though that implies some pressure!) that teaching an appreciation of other races and cultures really can be fun. Children are curious and especially enjoy having their curiosity satisfied. And when you consider that their satisfaction can include a wide range of colors, events, people, battles, friendships, foods, flags, inventions, actors and actresses, singing, dancing, tools, animals, clothes . . . What an experience!

As a parent, you are in a unique position. If you choose to, you can have the best of both worlds: You can prepare your child for a multicultural society and participate in the pleasures of learning, both yours and your child's. What a wonderful way to connect.

10

A Rainbow of Friends

Remember what it was like as a child when you wanted to do something but you held back because you were afraid others might laugh at you? or resent that you took initiative? Some examples we think of are hesitating to be the first one out on the floor during a school dance, making friends with the new kid on the block and risking jealousy among your longtime friends, and trying to make yourself invisible so the teacher wouldn't call on you to begin a series of oral reports.

Some of you had the courage and confidence to just do it. But for the rest of us, the experience was made a whole lot easier when we knew others felt the same way and there was a combined willingness to try something new or different together. Go out on that dance floor with three of your friends—strength in numbers!

Even though we're now grown-ups, and in many cases parents and teachers, taxpayers and homeowners, there is still a reluctance to try something different alone. We look around and feel much better when friends, neighbors, or role models join in or are already leading the way. This is also true with appreciating America's cultural diversity.

Do you feel awkward among your peers or unsure about what can be done in your school and community? Fine, if you do. Millions of us have similar feelings.

The good news is you don't have to start from scratch, because increasingly across the country people are involved in efforts to promote a better understanding and appreciation between diverse racial groups. The vast majority of efforts are small ones—people working in their own homes, schools, blocks, neighborhoods, and villages and towns. No one's asking you to change society, but we do ask that you do what you can to be part of efforts to make the change peaceful and rewarding.

Being involved is also an excellent way to prepare your child for a multicultural society. Much better than climbing on a soapbox is to have your youngster observe the practical ways you are putting good intentions into action. A great beginning is to see how people and programs are making a difference. One or more of the following ideas can be adapted for your community or child's school.

• Finley Junior High School in Huntington, New York, formed a Multicultural Action Committee (MAC), which we described in Chapter 6. It's a wonderful program that can be imitated in elementary as well as junior high schools.
• An annual event, called Calling All Colors, was begun in January 1992 in Myrtle Beach, South Carolina. It's a conference on racism with talks and demonstrations geared toward its audience of third-through eighth-graders. What's especially remarkable about this program is that it was organized by a nine-year-old, Anisa Kintz.
• The parents who send their children to Merricat's Castle Nursery School on the Upper East Side of Manhattan were concerned that the two dozen children enrolled were all white and thus had no opportunity to play and learn in a multicultural environment. The $11,000-per-student tuition was too steep for families in nearby neighborhoods. So the parents dug deeper into their own pockets for a scholarship program to pay for children of other backgrounds to attend. Now, one-third of the enrollment is African American and Latino.
• Several schools in suburban communities on Long Island (New York) have formed conflict-resolution teams consisting of students who air out differences before they escalate. One combined effort of these teams is to create a series of theatrical productions, with the plays portraying various situations involving white, black, Latino, and Asian students.

Among the situations portrayed: Two adolescents, a white boy and a black girl, would like to see each other outside of school but face intense peer and parental pressures; an Asian family moves into an all-white community, provoking hatred in otherwise perfectly normal people; when a youngster at a party objects to racial slurs, the other party-goers turn their ridicule on him. The schools also sponsor talks to the students, one of them given by jazz saxophonist Branford Marsalis, who told anecdotes of his Southern upbringing.

• Schools around the country are adopting the 3M program—multiracial, multiethnic, and multicultural education—which began in September 1991 at the Prospect Middle School in Pittsburgh and has since received funding from the U.S. Department of Education.

Teachers who have received training to work with a multiracial student body and/or a multicultural approach to learning stress to youngsters the contributions of many racial and ethnic groups. Some examples of curriculum changes are these: Art classes mix workshops on African masks with African history lessons; social studies units on freedom include the struggles of Chinese students, Nelson Mandela, and Eastern Europeans; and science classes read up on the achievements of an international list of Nobel Prize winners. The Pittsburgh school reports an increase in grades and a decrease in truancy and racial incidents.

• A minister in one northeast suburban community refused to confirm a group of adolescents after hearing them utter racially derogatory remarks. By questioning the youngsters, she learned that their attitudes were derived from their parents. With the support of her church, the minister postponed confirmation until youngsters and their parents attended racial-sensitivity workshops.

• Ellen Smith Bigelow—the director of Common Ground, a program in Hartford, Connecticut, that tries to bridge racial and economic boundaries—operates after-school gatherings of youngsters of various ages who work on community projects and form discussion groups to share their feelings on differences and tensions between people of diverse backgrounds.

• Over two dozen school districts in suburban Suffolk County, New York, are participating in the new BUTY program—Bring Unity to Youth. Students are brought on field trips to museums to see multicultural exhibits, attend lectures and seminars, and form discussion groups to express their feelings about racial incidents that earn local and national headlines.

• Elementary school teachers in Pasadena, California, have formed an interracial task force to develop an antibias curriculum. The lesson plan includes having children spend several days with an Asian doll and talking about how people look different and speak different languages. Teachers use the doll to describe how bad it feels when people make unpleasant remarks about her features.

• Kathleen and James McGinnis of St. Louis are the founders of the Institute for Peace and Justice. Among its activities is offering parents ideas on what they can do in their home to promote an appreciation of diverse racial groups. Something they do in their own home is to have an African madonna in their living room and children's pictures of Jesus with youngsters of many colors.

• In the Sheepshead Bay section of Brooklyn a group of youngsters between the ages of eight and ten have formed the Mosaic Minstrels. The group, comprised from various racial backgrounds, travels to nearby schools to sing songs in several languages. In January 1993, the Mosaic Minstrels traveled by bus to Washington to take part in cultural activities celebrating the inauguration of President Bill Clinton.

• By order of Governor Jim Florio, several counties in New Jersey have formed human-relations commissions, consisting of parents, educators, and local officials, to discuss and seek solutions to racial and ethnic conflicts. The commissions are a result of bias incidents (against the Asian Indian community in one of the counties) that angered and embarrassed neighbors.

• Lorraine Omley, a sixth-grade teacher in St. Paul, Minnesota, has her class play two games, Lunch Buddies and The Friendly-Wed Game. In the first, her students eat lunch with other students of different racial backgrounds for a week, and then they are asked to tell the class a few of the more interesting things about the other students they that didn't know before. In the second, youngsters are assigned partners and required to find out about that partner's family, background, likes and dislikes. One outcome of these games is that in the school cafeteria, students no longer sit together based on race.

• The Brooklyn Children's Museum has expanded its Collections Connection program to include two special exhibits that teach youngsters how to research objects from African and Jewish traditions. The children not only discover the richness of both cultures but learn how discrimination has affected each group.

• In 1990, ten ninth-grade students in a global studies program at Longwood Junior High School on Long Island formed a group called

STAR—Students Together Against Racism. That group now has over two hundred members. Among their activities are camping trips during which students of various races discuss their concerns, describe their family backgrounds, and live together.

Another way to explore multiculturalism is to suggest that your company become involved in a growing national trend: diversity workshops. Some workplace experts predict that within the next few years, dealing with diversity at places of employment will become a multibillion-dollar industry.

It is estimated that 40 percent of American companies have some form of diversity training. One-fourth of some fourteen hundred companies polled last year by Haygroup of Philadelphia said that "adapting to work-force diversity" is "a priority." And of 645 national companies surveyed by Towers Perrin, 29 percent offered programs in managing diversity.

No doubt companies are offering racial-sensitivity programs for employees and their families because they realize demographic changes will result in a very different twenty-first-century workforce. One example is DuPont, based in Wilmington, Delaware, which makes programs available to its forty thousand employees nationwide (and strongly urges attendance), with an emphasis on how their children might be acquiring prejudiced attitudes.

Because it is, at the very least, good public relations, companies in your area that have such programs are usually willing to make community presentations. If you're not already aware of such a company or program, contact the American Society for Training and Development in Alexandria, Virginia (703-683-8129), and ask about its multicultural employee-training program.

What often prevents some people from getting involved in fostering an appreciation of racial diversity is pessimism. Such people think that nothing will make a difference or that small efforts won't make enough of a difference.

It is especially distressing when pessimism is expressed by young people. A survey conducted for People for the American Way (a civil rights group based in Washington, D.C.) reported in March 1992 that 50 percent of young people interviewed said the state of race relations in the U.S. was "generally bad." Nearly twelve hundred white, black,

Latino, and Asian youths were questioned. It's certainly a disturbing finding that half our young people feel this way.

It is also disturbing that many people believe racial conflict is inevitable. A New York Times/CBS News poll conducted in May 1992 found that a majority of those interviewed thought the violent rebellion in Los Angeles earlier that spring was only a "warning" of the violence to come. Respondents said the biggest difficulty was "a lack of knowledge and understanding of each other and how to solve the problems." Fifty-three percent of whites and 55 percent of blacks said "there will always be a lot of prejudice and discrimination in America."

And not by a longshot is the perception of problems confined to whites and blacks. In February 1992 the U.S. Commission on Civil Rights issued a report, "Civil Rights Issues Facing Asian Americans in the 1990s," revealing that even though the Asian American population in the United States is increasing and a significant number of people find them to be a "model minority," incidents of prejudice, discrimination, and violence against this group is soaring. (It's interesting and sad to note that the commission now has a staff of seventy-seven— less than one-third of its peak strength in the 1980s.)

A pessimistic attitude and these survey findings might lead us to think that we might as well throw our hands up, hope things don't get too bad, and warn ourselves to "stick with our own kind." By doing that, however, we ignore the road that leads to the peaceful coexistence of racial groups. Let's face the primary fact: We're all here, and we have to learn to live together or our children will be bequeathed a future of prejudice, conflict, and lost opportunities. By not taking this road, we risk a dysfunctional society that is too concerned with tensions to evolve into a more enlightened civilization.

Alas, we see especially distressing examples on a daily basis—the ethnic and racial conflicts that have destroyed the former nation of Yugoslavia and the tensions that have erupted in Czechoslovakia and several of its Eastern European neighbors, and in India. Unable and unwilling to live together, various factions are warring among themselves simply because of different backgrounds. Deliberately and in cross fires, thousands of innocent people have been slaughtered. It is highly unlikely this bloodletting will result in progressive, enriching societies.

Can it happen here? Well, why take a chance? More than that—

why not grow together and appreciate our cultural diversity? Rather than ignore or accept a clear and present danger, let us here and now take advantage of an opportunity never before available in any civilization in history to create a truly multicultural society that builds on the benefits millions of people can contribute. In the process, America once again can show the world that it is a leader and a beacon of light in the destructive turmoil that is racial and ethnic conflict.

No, you can't single-handedly change society. But good intentions and cooperation with like-minded people will construct a stronger foundation. As nationally syndicated columnist Sydney H. Schanberg wrote after the Los Angeles conflagration:

> *I don't know if America is capable of racial change. I just know that we have to try—not think about it, not talk about it, not just get temporarily outraged, but do something concrete to make a real start at bridging the immense gulf between the races.*

The only disagreement we have with Schanberg is the word "immense." The gulf is not immense; it is significant, but narrower than many people think. You will find this out as you strive for a better racial climate for your children and, in the process, encounter a rainbow of friends.

Who are these people? They are people like you—carpenters, taxi drivers, accountants, physicians, athletes, artists, plumbers, waitresses, editors, assembly-line workers, salespeople, small-business owners, musicians, electricians, unemployed or retired people, food vendors, teachers, and parents, all wanting the best for their children and the society their children will come of age in.

In many ways children show us the way. None are born prejudiced. These innocent beings are naturally curious and readily accepting of friendship and love. The November 1992 issue of *Jet* magazine published the results of a Louis Harris poll. Among the findings was that 73 percent of the over eight hundred children (age ten to fourteen) surveyed nationwide had a friend of a different race, and 67 percent would welcome a next-door neighbor of another race. (Sixty-eight percent said they acquired their racial attitudes from their parents.)

On almost a daily basis, we see the eagerness of children to accept differences. As we mentioned in a previous chapter, during one of the

Positive Play workshops that we do around the country we showed Shani, an African American fashion doll, to a group of children in a segregated, inner-city section of Chicago and asked if Shani could be friends or play with Barbie. Most of the children said no. When we asked the same question of children in a highly integrated section of Los Angeles, they answered with a resounding yes. Several of the children explained, "It didn't matter if they were black or white, but how they felt about each other." It's obvious to us that color is not a significant consideration among children who are given the opportunity to interact.

We were particularly touched by an essay written by Jason C. Deuchler, an eighth-grader in Illinois who has a black mother and a white father, after the Los Angeles upheaval. In it he wrote:

> *I think the whole thing is that some people are scared and confused. . . . They don't appreciate people of other cultures and groups. Knowing different kinds of people makes your life more interesting and fun. We all just need to talk and take more time to understand one another and not let every little thing get on our nerves. People should not be afraid of each other just because they are different.*

Children are so open and accepting of people and experiences. They don't judge a person or difference as bad unless taught or influenced to do that. If encouraged to retain their openness and acceptance, they won't have a problem with caring for and appreciating peers of other colors. Colors are interesting and fun. When bias is absent, colors do not determine a person's worth or goodness. Children have that wonderful, natural ability to believe that whatever new thing they encounter is probably good unless proven otherwise. In this regard they know more than we do, and we don't help them by teaching otherwise.

All of us, when we face situations that inspire fear or concern or mistrust, look for support and solace from others. It's there for you. A rainbow of friends is available next door, down the street, in your neighborhood, in the school district, in your community.

The tide is turning. Be part of it. Teach your children well, prepare them for a multicultural society, and give the next generation a real chance to enjoy and benefit from what all of us have to offer.

Part IV

Folktales

INTRODUCTION

Why do we read stories? Two reasons are to be entertained and to have our imaginations stimulated. Most of us can quickly recall stories or novels that made us care about the characters and their fates. Even now, in the age of television and video, we find satisfaction in a good book that fills us with concern about the people on the page and prompts us to think about issues outside our own lives.

Another reason is that many stories carry the basic tenets of our culture. We want to record our traditions, beliefs, practices, and hopes. Much of what we know about humankind's earliest civilizations is from cave paintings, spoken epic poems that were handed down from generation to generation (Homer's *Iliad* is one example), and tales painstakingly inscribed on stone tablets. It is important to every society to spread its culture and to try to preserve it for the future.

Why do we read stories to our children? Well, they help kids relax for sleep! But beyond that, we choose stories that will entertain and inform. In a relaxing way, stories teach children about our own culture and the values we want to impart to them.

We present these folktales from several cultures for two reasons. The first is that we think they are interesting stories that children will enjoy. Some are very short, others are more involved. We ask that you decide which ones are the most age-appropriate in your home.

The second reason is that these stories provide a window through which your children, and maybe you, too, can gain an understanding of other cultures. We haven't included tales of the Grimm brothers or other familiar stories because they are too well known and generic. The tales offered here are from different parts of the world, provide views of how other people live and what has influenced them, and you may not have encountered them before.

We have attempted to present a diversity of cultures, yet one aspect that struck us is the common threads our various traditions have. For example, our conception of the creation of the world may not be exactly the same as those in Asia or India or Africa, but it's remarkable how many similar elements there are. Language, tools, dress, food, and religious beliefs might differ by geography or culture, but it seems that every society that has ever inhabited this planet has valued kindness, honesty, love, hard work, intelligence, and tradition.

You would be unable to hold this book if we had tried to provide a comprehensive cross section of folktales. There are hundreds and probably thousands available. We urge you to look some up in your local library or bookstore. True, some traditional tales convey gender or racial bias, and these should be avoided, or modified in the retelling. But many others are simply darn good stories about good people trying to overcome obstacles.

We hope you will read the stories here to your children or, if they are old enough, encourage them to read by themselves. Most likely, children will ask questions. Don't worry if you don't know the answers. Very few of us are experts on other cultures and their beliefs. Consider the questions as opportunities to further explore other cultures together.

The folktales, we think, demonstrate that whatever our skin color or cultural background, we share many if not all the same values that from the dawn of humankind have enabled civilization to progress. Offering stories is a subtle yet effective way of teaching children that the rainbow generation of the twenty-first century has much to appreciate, enjoy, and share.

The Earth on Turtle's Back

Onondaga Indians,
Northeast United States

Before the earth began, there was only water. It flowed as far as anyone could see. Birds and animals swam in the water.

Up in the clouds was Skyland. In this place in the air was a large and lovely tree with four long roots stretching out in four directions. All kinds of fruits and flowers grew on the tree's branches.

A family lived in Skyland, a woman who was expecting a child and her husband. One night, the woman dreamed that the large tree was uprooted. She told her husband about the dream. After she finished he said, "This dream makes me sad. Dreams are very powerful, and this one is telling us that the Great Tree must be uprooted."

The husband called together other men who lived in Skyland, and he instructed them to work together to uproot the tree. But the roots were so deep and strong that they couldn't move it. Finally, the husband stepped to the tree and wrapped his arms around it. He pulled and tugged with all his strength. Suddenly, it came loose. He laid the tree on its side.

Now, however, there was a big hole in Skyland. Filled with curiosity, the wife bent over to look down through the hole, grabbing one of the tree's branches for balance. Far, far below she saw glittering water. Ever more curious, she leaned farther . . . and fell through the hole! As her hand slipped off the branch, it was filled with seeds. Down she fell, tumbling through the air.

Several birds and animals paused in their swimming to look up. "Someone is falling from the sky!" exclaimed one of the birds.

"We must help her," another bird said.

Two swans spread their wings and lifted off the water. They caught the woman and gently brought her down to the water.

"She's not like us," one of the animals observed. "See, no webbed feet. I bet she can't live in the water."

Another animal asked, "What should we do?"

"I have an idea," said one of the birds. "I've heard that there is earth below the water. If we dive down and get some, then she can stand on it."

This seemed like a wise thing to do, and the woman thanked the birds and animals for their help. One by one they dove under the water—first a duck, then a beaver, then a loon. But each one came up without any earth. They groaned with disappointment.

Then a small voice was heard: "I will bring up some earth."

The animals saw that it was a tiny muskrat who spoke. She took a deep breath and dove below. Down, down, down she went into the cold, murky water. Though small and not very strong, the muskrat refused to give up. It became so dark that she couldn't see and her lungs burned, yet she kept diving deeper. Finally, when she thought she couldn't swim anymore, the muskrat's paw felt the bottom, grasped some earth, and swiftly rose to the surface.

The animals and birds were delighted to see earth in the muskrat's paw. But there was a new problem. "Where do we put it?" one asked.

A deep voice offered, "Put it on my back." It was a large turtle who lived below the surface.

The muskrat placed her paw on the turtle's back and placed the small amount of earth on it. (Today you can still see the scratch marks on a turtle's shell made by the muskrat's paw.) Instantly, the earth began to spread, growing wider and deeper until it covered much of the world.

The two swans carefully put the woman down. She opened her hand and the seeds fell to the ground. From those seeds, trees and grass grew.

And this is how life on earth began.

Banh Giay and Banh Chung

VIETNAM

King Hung-Vuong was an old man who had worked hard all his life to bring peace and safety to the people of Vietnam. He decided the time had come to retire.

The king had twenty-two sons. He had to choose one of these princes to become king. But the decision was difficult because they were all fine sons. After a great deal of thought, he came up with the idea of sending them all on a journey.

After calling them together he announced, "Go roam the earth and find for me foods I haven't tasted. The one who returns with the best food will become king."

They prepared for their journeys and then set off to the east, west, north, and south—all, that is, except one young prince named Lang Lieu. He didn't even leave the palace! He was sad because he didn't know where to go to find a special food for his father.

One night, a few weeks later, a genie appeared to Lang Lieu in a dream. The genie said, "Do not be sad and full of despair. I am here to help you. We'll start with rice, which everyone must eat to live."

The genie instructed the young prince to get some rice, beans, a bit of fat, pieces of pork, and spices. Next the prince plucked leaves from a banana tree and cut thin strips of bamboo.

When Lang Lieu had all these ingredients, the genie told him to make a stuffing of the bean paste and the pork pieces. Next Lang Lieu placed this mixture between layers of rice. This in turn he wrapped in banana leaves and pressed into the shape of square and round loaves. Each was then tied with the thin bamboo strips.

"Cook these cakes for a day and they will be ready to eat," the genie advised.

Soon afterward, the twenty-one princes returned from their journeys. Each had made a dish with ingredients found in far-off lands, and each expected to please his father and become king.

The dishes were brought before the king. He tasted each one, but each time he shook his head and frowned. Then Lang Lieu appeared and gently asked if he could present his dish. When the king nodded, the young prince offered him the cakes he had prepared. The king looked at them with curiosity. He'd never seen anything like them before, yet they looked delicious.

The king took a bite from the round loaf. Then he ate all of it. He ate the square cake. Then he asked for more. Lang Lieu produced other cakes he had baked. The king ate every cake!

"How did you make them?" the king asked, smacking his lips.

His son told him the story of the genie in the dream. The king was impressed. He thought that if Lang Lieu had such a dream, which helped him to make such a wonderful food, his son must have special powers, and thus would be a good king. He declared that Lang Lieu was now king.

Just before he passed his crown to his son, the old king decreed that the round loaf be called Banh Giay and the square one Banh Chung and that the recipe should be given to all the people of Vietnam.

And that is how, to this day, these two foods are tasty favorites of the Vietnamese people and are served on special occasions in many homes.

The Flight of the Animals

INDIA

In a grove of coconut and carob trees, near the Bay of Bengal, lived a short-eared rabbit so timid that he went out only at night to search for food.

One day, though, the rabbit was especially hungry, so he crawled out of his burrow while the sun was still up in the sky. It was a warm, peaceful day, and after a few minutes the rabbit decided to rest in a warm pool of sunlight by a carob tree.

The rabbit sighed with contentment, gazing up at the patches of sky between the oval leaves and the dark brown seed pods hanging from the branches. These pods contained pulp as sweet as honey, and the rabbit hoped one would drop to the ground for his supper.

But then he had a terrible thought: What would happen if one day the sky itself fell? Where could he possibly go for protection? His burrow . . . but if the sky fell, that could cause an earthquake and the ground would collapse! The timid rabbit became more and more frightened as these awful thoughts raced through his mind.

Just then, a hard-shelled coconut came loose, fell through the air, and landed with a loud, thundering crash. In complete panic, the rabbit jumped up, and without a glance behind he ran as fast as his little legs would go.

He passed a long-eared hare who called out, "Why are you running so fast?"

The rabbit didn't stop, so the hare caught up with him and asked his question again. "The earth is caving in!" the terrified rabbit gasped.

Immediately, the hare became just as scared. They ran together, and were soon joined by more hares and rabbits, until there were hundreds running together.

Two deer in a clearing nervously watched the creatures approach.

"What's the matter?" they called. When they were told the earth was collapsing, they too began to run.

The creatures encountered a rhinoceros, who asked the same question. When he too heard the answer, he started to rumble along.

Within minutes, the group of running animals had grown to include bears, elks, wild oxen, gnus, jackals, monkeys, tapirs, camels, tigers . . . and even big, strong elephants!

A lion, standing at the foot of a mountain, spotted the fleeing animals. He climbed onto a rock and roared, his voice sounding so ferocious and echoing in the valley that all the animals suddenly stopped. "Why are you all running?" the lion roared, this time not as loud.

In one voice the animals replied, "The earth is collapsing behind us."

"Really?" mused the lion. "Who saw this?"

"The tigers," said the elephants. "Ask them."

"Actually, we didn't see it," the tigers admitted. "But the camels did."

"Uh, we didn't quite see it," the camels murmured. "But you can ask the tapirs."

Well, the tapirs pointed to the monkeys, who pointed to the jackals, who pointed to the oxen, who . . . Finally, the long-eared hare was singled out, who pointed to the short-eared rabbit.

"So, did *you* see the earth collapse?" asked the lion. His fierce stare made the rabbit more terrified than ever.

"Yes. I mean, I think so," replied the rabbit. "I was in a grove of coconut and carob trees, just minding my own business and relaxing in the sunshine, when suddenly there was a huge crash and I took off."

"Show me where this happened," the lion demanded.

"I'm too scared to go there," squeaked the rabbit.

"Nothing to be afraid of when I'm around," the king of beasts insisted. "Here, climb on my back."

Together, they traveled to the grove where the rabbit had rested. Right away the lion saw the large coconut that had fallen to the ground, its hard shell split. It was obvious to him that it had created the loud crash. The lion escorted the embarrassed rabbit back to his burrow. Then he returned to the gathering of trembling animals at the foot of the mountain and explained to them that they had nothing to fear.

The animals went back to their homes. They didn't realize that if the lion had not stopped the stampede, they would have run right into the bay and drowned.

Cinder Jack

One morning, a farmer sent the oldest of his three sons out to guard his field. The boy munched on a cake as he stood among the crops. Suddenly, a frog hopped close and asked for a piece of cake. "Get out of here!" the boy snarled, throwing a rock at the frog.

The frog went away. Made drowsy by the sunlight and warm breeze, the boy fell asleep. When he woke he discovered that all the crops had withered and died.

The next day, the farmer sent out his second son to guard another field he owned. This boy also angrily chased the frog away, and after his nap, he found this field too contained only dead crops.

The farmer was furious, and he feared his one last field would become useless. Then his youngest son, who was nicknamed Cinder Jack because he quietly sat by the fireplace, offered to guard the third field. His father and brothers laughed at him. They didn't think he could do anything right. But they let him go out to the field, nibbling on a sweet cake.

This time, when the frog appeared and asked for a piece of cake, Jack immediately gave him one. The frog was grateful and admired the boy's kindness and generosity. The young man was given three rods—one copper, one silver, and the last made of gold. The frog told him that three horses would soon arrive and try to trample the crops in the remaining field, but if Jack held up the rods the horses would be tamed and be at his command.

Later that day, the horses appeared, and Jack did as the frog advised. As the weeks passed the crops grew tall and full, and the farmer reaped an excellent harvest. Jack never revealed what had happened. As he usually did, he stayed quietly by the fireplace.

One Sunday, the king had a pole erected in front of the palace with a flower made of gold tied to the top. He announced that whoever could pluck the flower with one jump from horseback could marry his daughter. All the knights in the kingdom tried, and each one failed.

Suddenly, a knight wearing copper armor and a copper helmet and riding a copper horse appeared at the palace. With one leap he snatched the flower, then rode away.

The king was amazed and wondered who the copper knight could be. The next Sunday he had a higher pole, with a golden apple atop it, erected. Again, dozens of knights tried, and all failed. This time a knight wearing silver armor and a silver helmet and riding a silver horse arrived. He grabbed the apple, then rode away.

On the third Sunday the king had a silk handkerchief laced with gold threads attached to the top of an even higher pole. Only a few knights tried for it; the rest had given up. Then a knight in gold armor and gold helmet and riding a gold horse showed up, took the handkerchief, then galloped away.

That night the farmer and his two oldest sons discussed the amazing events at the palace. When Jack tried to join the discussion, they told him to be quiet, that he wasn't worthy of discussing such things.

The king guessed that the knights in copper, silver, and gold armor were all the same person. He decreed that the knight should present himself—with the flower, apple, and handkerchief—and become his son-in-law. But no one came to the palace. Filled with wonder, the king ordered that every man should come to the palace.

Observing the men standing in the courtyard, the king couldn't find the knight. Then he appeared, wearing gold armor and a gold helmet and riding a gold horse. The knight leaned over and gave the princess the flower, the apple, and the handkerchief and respectfully asked her to be his wife.

The king and all the people shouted with joy. Bells were rung and cannons fired. But everyone was astonished when the knight removed his helmet and they saw he was Cinder Jack!

The young man married the princess and helped the king govern the land. Jack was so good-hearted that he built a new house for his brothers and brought his father to live with him. When the king died, Jack became king and ruled for many years, teaching his subjects the value of generosity and kindness.

How the Porcupine
Outwitted the Fox

HONDURAS

A very long time ago porcupines were not prickly. They had soft fur like some other animals. One day, though, the porcupine's appearance changed forever.

A family of porcupines lived in a large forest. They were very shy and lived by themselves, but because they had each other they were happy.

One summer evening Mr. and Mrs. Porcupine were returning from dinner. They had feasted on the tender twigs and bark of a poplar tree. They looked forward to the whole family having a peaceful night's rest.

Suddenly, Mr. Porcupine stopped in his tracks. He lifted his nose to the breeze. Then he smiled. "I smell fresh clover!" he happily exclaimed. "Come, dear. Let's go eat some."

"We've just had a fine meal," his wife pointed out. "And you know hungry foxes hide in the tall grass of the meadow. Please, let's just go home."

"You go on if you wish," Mr. Porcupine offered. "By this time foxes have returned to their homes. I'll just go to the meadow, nibble a bit of clover, and be right back."

"All right," sighed his wife. "But be careful."

Mr. Porcupine made his way to a nearby meadow and there he began to nibble the fresh clover he found. Then he nibbled some more. And more. The clover was so delicious, and there was so much of it, that he couldn't stop stuffing it into his mouth. He wasn't aware that his feeding frenzy was taking him deeper into the meadow.

"What was that?" he whispered to himself. He'd heard some movement close by. His eyes searched the tall grass surrounding the meadow. The moon emerged from behind a cloud, and in its pale light the porcupine saw a shadow creeping through the meadow.

"It's a fox!" he gasped. Terrified, he looked for a tall tree to climb, but there was none in the meadow. The shadow drew closer. No time to dig a hole for safety!

"Please help me, Noh Ku," Mr. Porcupine begged, addressing the great god of the land. "Don't let the fox eat me. Oh, poor me!"

As Mr. Porcupine cringed with fear, the shadow approached. He squeezed his eyes shut, unable to bear the sight of the famished fox. Suddenly, a cold chill swept through his body. Something strange was happening to his fur.

The fox emerged from the tall grass. He licked his lips at the sight of the lone porcupine. Ah, what a tasty treat! He leaped at the porcupine . . . then the startled fox howled in pain. Astonished and hurt, the fox turned and ran away, into the forest.

After a few moments, Mr. Porcupine opened his eyes. "How am I still alive?" he whispered in amazement. Then he understood that somehow Noh Ku had answered his plea for help. He hurriedly waddled home.

Mrs. Porcupine waited nervously. She'd heard the howl of pain and she feared her husband would not return. But when he appeared in the doorway, she cried with relief—then screamed with surprise at what he looked like.

"What has happened to your beautiful brown fur?" she asked.

Mr. Porcupine had no idea what she was talking about.

"Let's go to the pond where you can see your reflection in the moonlit water," his wife suggested.

When he peered into the pond, Mr. Porcupine understood: His fur had become thousands of tall, pointy-tipped quills. What a gift from Noh Ku! Now he could go to the meadow in search of food anytime he wished.

He was extremely happy . . . until he saw his wife's face. She was not pleased at all.

"Aren't you glad for this strong protection I have against the fox?" he asked.

"Of course," she replied. "But I am not like you. We cannot hunt for food together. And," she added, wiping away tears, "you are not a porcupine anymore."

Mr. Porcupine felt sad, too. He thought that because of his gluttony, Noh Ku had actually punished him. What could he do now? Then he happened to glance in the water.

"Dear, look at yourself!" he cried.

She did. And she saw that now she too had lovely brown quills like her husband's. Her face beamed with joy.

"This night, Noh Ku has given our whole family protection," Mr. Porcupine concluded.

It was true. Returning home, they saw their children covered with quills. And whenever they encountered other porcupines, they looked the same. From that night to the present day, porcupines have been able to forage for food without fear of foxes and other large animals.

Simon and the Big Joke

TRINIDAD

The day before my birthday, Tantie came over to help Mama bake a cake and pies for my party. My brothers Avril and Cedric and my sister Susan and I gathered around her as soon as she walked in and begged her to tell us a story.

She couldn't resist our request. Tantie said she'd tell us a story about a true event, a joke she played on someone. This is what she told us:

When my mama was ten, Tantie took her on a boat ride to Tobago. It was a big boat with many people standing on the deck watching the waves thud against the sides. Tantie and my mama noticed an old man with a monkey on his shoulder. It seemed like the man and the monkey were arguing. Then the man shouted, "I don't want this monkey any more! Anybody can have him for a dollar!"

One woman rushed over and gave him a dollar. Who wouldn't want a talking monkey? The man told her the monkey's name was Simon. The woman was overjoyed to have bought a prize so cheaply. She cradled the monkey in her arms and whispered softly to it.

"What?" Simon croaked.

The woman was astonished, as was the crowd around her. Then the monkey said, "If you're going to say something, say it so I can hear it!"

Well, this was a little too much. It's one thing for a monkey to talk, another for it to be rude. She wasn't sure she wanted to keep Simon.

Tantie was curious. She looked for the old man. He had stepped back from the crowd and was leaning against the railing, a big smile on his face. Tantie felt sorry for the woman. And then she felt even more sorry when the woman politely tried to get the monkey to say more but it refused to speak. Tantie squinted her eyes and thought.

She took my mama and the woman, who was still cradling Simon, downstairs to the dining room. They sat at a table and asked Simon questions, but he ignored them. Becoming restless, the monkey began to jump on the table and then leap all about, sticking its paws in people's hair. They were getting pretty angry.

The old man entered the dining room. He caught Simon and returned him to the woman. He said that for another dollar, he would take the rude monkey back.

"Take him back?" Tantie exclaimed. "What for? He's some monkey. Why, he's been talking a mile a minute."

"Oh, go on," the old man muttered, his eyes growing wide.

"It's the truth," Tantie said, winking at my mama. "We all heard him, right?"

"Clear as day," my mama said, winking back. "He told us he wanted bananas and mangoes for lunch."

"You heard him talk?" the old man gasped.

"Oh, yes, he's quite a talker," Tantie replied. "This nice woman here, she's going to be rich!"

"Now . . . now, wait a minute here," the old man said, his hands shaking. "Please, nice folks, you've got to see that Simon and I are longtime friends, and then we just had this tiny argument and . . . I was too quick to sell him. You're not really going to keep my friend from me, are you?"

"Well, you sold him fair and square for a dollar," Tantie said.

"That's true, but I was hasty." He reached into his pocket. To the woman he said, "Here's your dollar back."

"What!" Tantie cried. "Give up a talking monkey for the same dollar she gave you? She can make much more than that before she steps off this boat!"

The old man immediately realized this was true. Who wouldn't pay to see a monkey that could really talk? He reached deeper into his pocket. (All the while, my mama was almost bursting to laugh.) "All I have is five dollars," the man pleaded. "I'll gladly give it to you to have my friend Simon back."

Tantie nodded and the woman handed the monkey over. As they left the dining room, they saw the man talking to the monkey and then waiting for a response. Simon looked at him curiously, then yawned.

Tantie stopped her story. "But how can a monkey talk?" I asked.

"They can't, honey," Tantie said, her fingers brushing my cheek. "I figured out that old man knew how to throw his voice, like working a puppet, and make it seem as if anything could talk. That's how he made money, by fooling people. But he couldn't fool Tantie. No one can!"

We believed her . . . for a few minutes. Then my brothers and sister and I ran outside and climbed the mango tree. We hid behind the large leaves. We tried not to laugh when we saw Tantie come to the tree to pick mangoes for the pies. Soon as she touched one Avril cried, "Ow! Please missus, don't pick me!"

Tantie nearly fell down. She reached for another mango. "I don't want to be in a pie!" I pleaded.

Tantie screamed and ran for the house. No matter how hard we laughed, we could still hear our mama's laughter filling the house.

The Man Whose Luck
Was Sleeping

PERSIA

Many years ago there were two brothers who had each inherited half of their father's farm. The older brother worked hard day after day, but nothing would grow on his land. The younger brother seemed to barely work at all, yet his crops grew tall and plentiful.

The older brother thought about this, then decided that at night he would sneak into the other field, take some of the corn, and spread it on his property. So that night he brought a sack to the field, but just as he was about to fill it with corn a strange man appeared and asked him what he was doing.

"None of your business," the older brother said. "And who are you?"

"I'm your brother's Luck," the stranger replied. "I make sure nobody steals his corn."

"Very nice," the older brother mused. "I'd like to know where my Luck is."

The stranger told him that his Luck slept at the top of a mountain that was far away and that he would have to go there and wake it up. Thrilled at the prospect of finally having full fields, the older brother set off on the journey.

But before he reached the mountain, he was confronted by a huge lion who roared hungrily. The older brother trembled with fear. He fell to his knees and begged the lion to spare his life.

"Okay," the lion said. "I'll let you go on if you tell me where you're going and why."

After the younger brother told him about the search for his Luck, the lion said, "Here's my offer. I'll let you live if, when you find your Luck, you ask him why, no matter how much I eat, my belly never feels full, and if there's anything I can do about it."

The older brother gratefully agreed and continued on his journey. When night arrived he met an old farmer who allowed him to sleep at his house. As they ate supper the older brother told his story, that he was trying to find his Luck and wake it up.

The farmer said, "When you have found your Luck and wakened it, please ask why one of my fields never grows crops, no matter how many seeds I plant."

The older brother agreed. The next morning he renewed his journey and traveled until he came to the gates of a city. Guards brought him to see the king. At the king's request, the older brother told his story, that he needed to find and waken his Luck.

The king said, "When you've found your Luck, please ask why, no matter how much I try to be a good king, my people are always poor. How can I help them?"

After promising to ask this question, the older brother continued his trek. Soon he saw the mountain, and then he was slowly climbing up its slopes. At the top he found a large man lying on the ground, sound asleep.

"Wake up!" the older brother shouted.

The man's eyes opened. He stretched and yawned. "Okay, I'm awake now," he said. "What do you want?"

The older brother asked the questions from the lion, the farmer, and the king. The man told him the answers, and the older brother began his return journey.

When he was brought before the king, he asked the older brother if he'd asked the question.

"Yes," the older brother said.

"And what was the answer?"

The older brother leaned over and whispered, "My Luck said that you are really a woman, and your land will not prosper because you have deceived your people."

Shamefully, the king admitted this was true; then he offered to marry the older brother, who would become king, and they would rule together.

"I'm sorry, but I must get back to my home," the older brother said. The king wished him a safe journey, and the traveler went on his way.

When he encountered the farmer, the older brother told him that nothing would grow in his field because there was treasure buried beneath it. Once the farmer dug up the treasure, the field would be fertile.

The farmer grabbed shovels and together they dug in the field. Sure enough, they found treasure—seven jars filled with gold!

"You have done a wonderful thing for me," the farmer said. "Please stay here and share this treasure."

"I'm sorry, but I must get back to my own home," the older brother responded. "Now that my Luck is awake, I expect to have a great harvest in *my* field." And bidding the farmer good-bye, he resumed his trip home.

He was nearing home when suddenly the lion leaped into his path. The older brother told him of his adventures and that his Luck was awake.

"And how did he answer my question?" the lion asked.

Feeling full of importance, the older brother revealed, "Whenever you meet a man who is a complete fool, you should immediately tear him to pieces and swallow him."

The lion thought about this. Here the older brother had just told him he had refused becoming a king and sharing in treasure, and now he was confronting a hungry lion. "Well," the lion said, "I must say I never met a man more foolish than you!"

And that was the end of the older brother.

Two Tales from Haiti

The Origin of Lamps

Very, very long ago, the sky was close to the earth. When it was nighttime, people did not need candles or lamps or any form of illumination, because the stars shone nearby with a soft blue light.

Also at this time there was a very tall woman. Even when she sat down, her head was higher than the peaks of mountains!

One morning the woman was sweeping her front steps. The clouds decided to have fun by tickling her neck and ears. But the woman was annoyed by their playfulness.

"Leave me alone," she insisted. "Can't you see I'm busy?"

The clouds giggled and kept up the tickling and then scooted around her head, tickling her nose and mouth and covering her eyes. These tricks made the woman sneeze and cough.

"Better stop that," the woman warned, "or I'll be after you with this broom!"

The clouds only laughed harder at this and teased her even more.

That was it. The woman took a mighty swipe at the clouds with her broom. The clouds hurried out of harm's way. The sky became frightened and moved away, rising higher and higher up until it was far from the threatening broom. To be on the safe side—and enjoying being so high up—the sky chose to stay there.

But when the sun went down, there wasn't enough light for the people to see because the stars were no longer close by. So they invented lamps, and people have been using them at night ever since!

The Education of Goat

Many years ago, Cat and Goat were good friends. One day, Cat tried to teach his friend how to climb a tree.

This turned out to be very difficult, because Goat didn't have claws on his feet. Still, Goat kept at it and went a little farther up the tree every day. He found that by standing on his back legs and reaching up his front legs, he could reach the lower branches and nibble on their leaves.

Cat was pleased and encouraged his friend. "You're doing fine!" he called, while licking his fur. "You'll be climbing that tree in no time at all!" He offered Goat some more advice, then strolled away.

One morning, as Goat made another attempt, Cat came to watch and found Goat by the tree with Dog, who was also trying to learn how to climb. Cat was scared of Dog, and she leaped onto the roof of a hut.

"If you can teach Dog, then I guess you don't need any more lessons from me!" Cat shouted.

Cat decided to mind his own business from then on, and he stayed on the roof to warm himself in the sunlight.

And that is why, even though goats try from time to time, they will never manage to climb a tree.

Treasure Mountain

YAO PEOPLE, SOUTHERN CHINA

K'o-li and his mother lived in a small hut at the foot of a large mountain. Life was very hard because recently there had been an awful famine that had destroyed their crops of rice, soybeans, and wheat.

Every morning K'o-li hiked into the woods to a giant cathaya tree. With his bare hands he dug deep into the ground for the roots of the turtle foot plant next to the tree. This was hard work but K'o-li didn't mind, because his mother would steam the pulp of the roots and they would eat it for dinner. As they ate, K'o-li and his mother thanked the gods for the beauty surrounding them and for the turtle foot plant.

But one day when K'o-li went into the woods and then to the cathaya tree, he could find only a few tiny roots of the plant, no matter how much his fingers clawed at the earth. He was sad when he returned to the hut, yet he insisted that his mother have all of the little food there was.

"I'm not that hungry," he said.

"You are young and need your strength," said his mother. "I cannot survive without you, so please eat what we have."

There was a knock on the door. There stood an old man, his skin wrinkled and pale. He leaned on a walking stick, and it seemed he was too exhausted to go any farther.

"Oh, you must be starving!" exclaimed K'o-li's mother. "Please, come in and rest."

The old man looked at them but didn't speak.

The woman whispered to her son, "We have been debating who should eat this small portion of food. Perhaps we should give it to this poor old man."

K'o-li agreed, helped the old man to a chair, and gave him the food.

In only a minute, the bowl was empty. He then stood and started to leave, his legs quivering.

"Wait," K'o-li said. "I'm worried you will not make it home. Let me carry you."

K'o-li fetched a basket and strapped it onto his back. The old man climbed in, and the two set off.

"Which way?" K'o-li asked.

The old man pointed to the peak of the mountain. It was very high up, and the man wasn't too light, but K'o-li had vowed to help, and so he started climbing. The sun set and night came. K'o-li kept on, bearing the weight of the silent old man. Finally, as the sun was rising, they came to a large stone cave where the old man lived. K'o-li sighed with relief as he lowered the basket.

Just then, a girl with black hair and skin the texture of silk emerged. "Grandfather!" she cried. "I was so worried about you!"

The old man smiled and spoke at last. "Mi-mi, this young man gave me his last bit of food and then carried me home, and he never once complained about the good deed he was doing for me. Give him your earrings."

The girl took off her earrings, and they magically turned into keys! She said to K'o-li, "On the right side of this cliff is Treasure Mountain, and in it is a huge stone cave. Put the gold key into the stone door and it will open. Take all the treasure you want. When you're ready to leave, insert the silver key and the door will open again so you can get out. Make sure you don't lose the silver key or you will be trapped in the cave forever."

K'o-li stared in amazement at the two keys in his hand. When he looked up, the old man and the girl had disappeared!

K'o-li went off to his right and found the stone cave. He put the gold key into the lock and the door began to open. K'o-li stepped inside. The door closed behind him.

Inside, piled on the floor, were more treasures than the boy had ever imagined in his wildest dreams: gold coins, pearls, diamonds, gems of all kinds. But K'o-li was modest and not a bit greedy. He knew he would be content to work for his money, so he took only a stone grinder. "I can make a good living with this," he thought. He opened the door with the silver key and went back down the mountain.

K'o-li's mother was very proud of her son. He had displayed wisdom. Curious, she lifted the lid of the grinder. Suddenly, soybeans spilled out, thousands of them!

No matter how long the mother and son lived, they could not possibly eat all these beans, so K'o-li filled his basket and went to his hungry neighbors, giving each a large portion of beans.

Of course, a miracle like this couldn't remain a secret. Word spread fast through the valley. When the king heard of the amazing events, he sent soldiers to K'o-li's hut. They were very rude, and they left with the stone grinder.

The king was overjoyed to have the grinder. But when he went to lift the lid, the grinder turned to dust!

Back at the hut, K'o-li's mother asked, "Do you still have the two keys?"

"Yes," her son replied.

"Then please return to Treasure Mountain. It's not too much to ask for another tool that will help feed us and our poor neighbors."

K'o-li hiked back up to the top of the mountain. He opened the stone door with the gold key. Again, his eyes were nearly blinded by the glittering treasures. But again, he took only a simple tool, a stone mortar, and he returned to the hut.

Seeing the mortar, his mother started to pound at it with a wooden pestle. Suddenly, white rice began to tumble out. The more she pounded, the more rice came out. Another miracle! Once again, K'o-li strapped on his basket and distributed rice to his neighbors.

The king heard of this miracle too. Once more he sent soldiers to the hut, and once more they rudely took the mortar away to the palace. But when the king touched it, the mortar instantly turned to dust. The king howled with rage and ordered that the soldiers be punished.

K'o-li went up to the top of Treasure Mountain a third time and returned with a hoe to use in the fields. In every spot of soil the hoe touched, a huge stalk of wheat grew! In less than an hour, there was enough wheat to feed everyone in the valley.

This time the king ordered that K'o-li himself be brought to the palace. The soldiers came and bound the young man hand and foot and dragged him away. K'o-li was tossed on the floor before the king, who had executioners standing on either side of the throne.

"Where do you get your magic tools?" the king demanded. "If you refuse to tell me, my executioners will cut off your head!"

K'o-li was very scared, but he tried to think clearly. Finally he said, "They come from the top of the mountain. This gold key unlocks the door to the treasure cave."

The king laughed with delight. "Give me that key," he commanded. "Now, guide us to this cave."

The king and his army followed K'o-li up the mountain. When they reached the cave, the king inserted the gold key. He and the army rushed in the instant the door opened.

Only K'o-li remained outside. He slowly backed away, hearing the shouts of greedy joy from within. In K'o-li's hand was the silver key. He watched as the stone door closed, then went home.

For several days the young man worked hard in his field with the magic hoe, and enough wheat was harvested that the people of the valley would never be hungry again. One night, though, K'o-li's mother noticed that her son looked sad, and she asked what was the matter.

"I feel bad that by giving the king the gold key, I've lost one of the girl's earrings," he said.

"You are right to feel that way toward someone who was so kind to us," his mother said. "We must go back up the mountain and ask for her forgiveness."

K'o-li strapped on the basket, filled with soybeans, rice, and wheat, and he and his mother made the long journey up the mountain. When they arrived at the top, they saw the old man and his granddaughter sitting at the cave.

K'o-li bowed to them and said, "I am sorry for losing the gold key."

The girl smiled and took the silver key from him. Instantly, it became an earring.

"We have brought this food to you," K'o-li's mother said to the old man. "This is all we could carry. Please accept it as our gift to you."

"I do not need your food," the old man said kindly. "Please give it to your neighbors. But my granddaughter needs a good, honest, hardworking husband. I think K'o-li fits that description."

The old man smiled and bowed to them, then walked right through the mountain and vanished!

K'o-li, his mother, and the young woman returned to the hut, and several days later there was a marriage, celebrated by everyone in the valley. K'o-li continued to work the field with his hoe, and to this day there has been no more famine.

It is said that if you climb one of the mountains you will come to a cave with a large stone door. Behind that door is an enormous treasure. But no one will ever reap this treasure, because there is no key.

The Baby Leopard

WEST AFRICA
by Linda and Clay Goss

Once upon a time—a very long time ago—there lived a Baby Leopard. In those days, Leopards lived in houses, wore shoes, and told each other stories.

One day Baby Leopard wanted to go out and play. So he asked, "Mama, may I go outside and play?"

"Oh, yes, you may, my son. But I want you to remember one thing," said Mama Leopard . . .

"Baby Leopard, Baby Leopard, please don't mess with Fire!"

"But, Mama," said Baby Leopard, "I'm not afraid of Fire. I am a Leopard. Grrrrrrrrrrrrrrrrrowl."

Baby Leopard ran out into the bright sunshine.

He was having a wonderful time.

He chased the butterflies.

He chased the birds.

He chased the bees.

The leaves on the trees and the breeze could see Baby Leopard. They wanted to help him, so they whispered:

"Baby Leopard, Baby Leopard, please don't mess with Fire!"

But Baby Leopard looked up at them and said in an angry voice, "Who are you? You can't tell me what to do. I'm not afraid of any old Fire. I am a Leopard. Grrrrrrrrrrrrrrrrrrrowl!"

Baby Leopard would not listen.

Instead he kept on playing.

Until he began to smell a strange odor.

He didn't really know what the smell was.

Then he saw smoke.

Suddenly a giraffe with a very long neck appeared from the smoke. He was very frightened. He tried to warn Baby Leopard, and so he said loudly:

"BABY LEOPARD, BABY LEOPARD,
PLEASE DON'T MESS WITH FIRE!"

Baby Leopard laughed at the giraffe and said, "Calm down! Who do you think you're talking to? I'm not afraid of Fire. I am a Leopard. Grrrrrrrrrrrrrrrrowl."

Baby Leopard would not listen.

So the giraffe with the very long neck ran past Baby Leopard. Many animals of the forest were running past him.

And soon Baby Leopard was all alone in the forest except for one thing.

Red, yellow, and *orange* fingers began poking through the smoke. Connected to the fingers was a flaming *red, yellow, orange* body connected to a flaming *red, yellow, orange* head. And out of the head came a long flaming *red, yellow, orange* tongue.

The Fire began to dance toward Baby Leopard, moving closer and closer to him, and it said in a scary voice:

"BABY LEOPARD, BABY LEOPARD,
I AM FIRE!"

Baby Leopard stood very still. He was so afraid of the Fire that he could not move. He looked into the Fire and thought to himself, What is Fire going to do to me?

Fire's long arms began to encircle frightened Baby Leopard. Suddenly it said, "Oh, Baby Leopard, wouldn't you like to play a game with me? Let us play a game of tag, shall we?"

"I will burn your head. I will burn your nose.

I will burn your knees, I will burn your toes.

Scratch, scratch, scratch! Baby Leopard.

I will burn all over your back.

Ha Ha Ha Ha Ha Ha Ha Ha Ha Ha," laughed Fire.

"Oh, oh, oh," cried Baby Leopard, and he ran home to his mama.

Mama Leopard was very happy to see Baby Leopard. She picked him up. She hugged him and rocked him. Then she put some cornstarch all over his body.

Three months passed, and Baby Leopard felt somewhat better. But when he looked at his body, he saw so many burnt places. He tried to rub them out, but they would not go away.

Baby Leopard ran out into the rain and said, "Rain, Rain, please wash these off me."

But the rain said, "Baby Leopard, I am sorry, I can wash your back, but I can never ever wash out your spots."

Ever since that day, Leopards have had spots to remind all of us of one thing . . .

"Baby Leopard, Baby Leopard,
Please don't mess with Fire."

Lon Po Po

CHINA

Many years ago, a woman and her three children lived in a cottage far out in the country. When the birthday of the children's grandmother arrived, their mother set off to visit her. The woman warned her children—whose names were Shang, Tao, and Paotze—to keep the cottage door shut, for she wouldn't return until morning.

The children believed they could take care of themselves quite well, but they forgot about the crafty wolf that lived nearby. That evening, disguising himself as an old woman, the wolf knocked on the door.

"It is Po Po, your grandmother," said the wolf. "Please let me in."

Shang, the oldest, said, "But Po Po, our mother has gone to your house."

"Oh, my goodness!" exclaimed the wolf. "Well, I might as well wait for her here."

"Why is your voice so low?" Shang asked.

"I have a cold," the crafty wolf replied. "Let me in out of the cold wind."

The children opened the door and the wolf entered. He blew out the candle, claiming the wind had done it, casting the room into darkness. The children were nervous. "Come now," the wolf said, "let us get into bed together so we can be warm."

The children crawled under the blanket with the wolf. "Ah, Tao and Paotze, you are so delicious . . . I mean, so plump and sweet."

Shang yawned and stretched, and as she did so she brushed against the wolf's tail. "Po Po, your foot is very hairy," the girl remarked.

"Oh no, I brought some strings to do some weaving."

Shang touched the wolf's claws. "Po Po, there are thorns on your hands."

"Oh no, I brought some nails to mend your shoes."

Shang was more suspicious. She got out of bed and lit the candle. In the moment before the wolf blew it out, Shang saw the hairy face. Shang was frightened, but she was also very smart. She kept her voice light and pleasant.

"Po Po, you must be starved after the long walk here," Shang said. "We'll go outside and get you some gingko nuts. They are soft and tender and perfectly delicious. You can lie in bed and eat all you want."

This sounded attractive to the wolf, and the children stepped out of the cottage. Immediately, Shang whispered that "Po Po" was really a wolf, and all three of them climbed to the top of the closest tree.

The wolf waited for the children to return, then grew impatient. He shouted for the children. When there was no response, he wandered out of the cottage. He spotted the children at the top of the tree.

"I am truly starved now," the wolf called. "How about dropping down some of those nuts?"

"But Po Po, they taste best when eaten directly from the tree," Shang called back.

"I can't climb that tree!" the wolf whined.

The wolf paced back and forth, drooling as he heard the children eating nuts and commenting on their wonderful taste. "I must have something to eat!" the wolf growled.

Smart Shang said, "Get the basket from the cottage and throw the rope up to us. We will pull you."

Almost maddened by hunger, the wolf did this and then sat in the basket. Shang began to pull it. Halfway up the tree, Shang let go and the wolf crashed to the ground. He howled in pain.

"I'm sorry, Po Po!" Shang called. "This time Tao will help me and we'll pull you all the way up."

The wolf tossed up the rope and sat in the basket again. Both children pulled. This time the basket was almost up to them when they let go. The wolf fell on his head and screamed louder.

"We're sorry!" Paotze called. "I will help, and this time we'll get you up here for sure to eat all you want."

The wolf considered what hurt worse, his head or the hungry ache in his belly. Growling, he tossed the rope up and sat in the basket one more time.

All three children tugged and tugged. Inch by inch the basket rose up. The wolf was drooling fiercely now. He vowed that when he got up to the top of the tree, he would eat the children first, then have the nuts for dessert. Oh, what a meal this would be! He licked his chops as he was drawn closer to the children, and he tried to decide which one he would swallow first.

The children gave one last tug, and the basket was next to them. The wolf reached out one hairy paw, showing his claws. "Now!" Shang cried, and they let the rope go.

Down, down, down went the wolf, tumbling and spinning in the air, bellowing angrily. There was a terrible crash. The children peered down from the tree. The wolf lay on the ground, still and silent.

"Po Po?" Shang called.

"Oh, wolf?" Tao shouted.

"Yoo-hoo!" sang Paotze.

Carefully, Shang went down the tree first. The wolf didn't stir. The other children descended. Silently, all three went into the cottage and locked the door. They didn't hear a sound from outside, and soon they fell into a peaceful sleep.

The next day, when their mother returned, the wolf was gone. After hearing the story from her children, the woman concluded that the wolf had had enough tricks played on him and, when he'd woken up, had run away. Never again would he bother this cottage!

The children laughed over how they had been more crafty than the wolf. For breakfast, they feasted on all the delicious food the real Po Po had sent them.

Resource Guide

Never before have there been as many support materials available to help you nurture children along the path of appreciating cultural diversity and promoting understanding between racial groups. There is so much material that we couldn't possibly list every item. However, we believe we can get you off to a good start by suggesting materials to enjoy with your children.

Often in this book we have stressed the importance of exploring the richness of other cultures. This need not be an academic exercise; it can be an adventurous and stimulating journey to discovery. The materials we suggest here are fun as well as illuminating. Some of them children can busy themselves with. But for the most part, these materials should be used by adults with youngsters. The information will expand young minds, and it's likely you will learn by seeing through a child's eyes.

We have divided this guide into two main categories. The first lists general sources that have a wealth of material available and are only too happy to respond to requests for catalogs describing the materials.

The second category is comprised of books, games and dolls, cassettes, and videos. When you inquire about or consider purchasing or borrowing these items from libraries, bookstores, toy shops or music outlets, please consider the age of your child. Offering your child an item that is significantly below or beyond his or her abilities can blunt its positive impact and lead to frustration or disinterest.

Salespeople are usually adept at suggesting appropriate products for your child's age range. And if you have more than one child, what pleases one might not work for the other; yet over time that item will be something they want to try. While children can use some of the materials independently, we still encourage parents, teachers, and other caregivers to be involved.

We have listed the items roughly according to age, from preschool through age twelve. (Catalogs you send for usually cite specific age ranges for their product.) Young children can enjoy books meant for an older audience if you read them aloud and explain the advanced terms.

We hope those in the education system will bring these materials into the classroom or create from them their own lists for students to take home. It would be especially helpful if the school acquired some of these materials and then made them available to students through its library, audio-visual department, and after-school programs.

General Sources

The National Association for the Education of Young Children puts out a pamphlet called "Teaching Your Children to Resist Bias" (50 cents; 100 copies for $10). Also available is "Anti-Bias Curriculum: Tools for Empowering Young Children," by Louise Derman-Sparks. Write to NAEYC, 1834 Connecticut Ave., NW, Washington, DC 20009, or call 800-424-2460.

The Council on Interracial Books for Young Children has a catalog of multicultural books. Write to 1841 Broadway, New York, NY 10023, or call 212-757-5339 for a copy.

The National PTA has a booklet titled "What to Tell Your Child About Prejudice and Discrimination." Request copies by calling 312-787-0977, or write to 700 North Rush St., Chicago, IL 60611-2571.

For materials on dealing with prejudice and discrimination contact the Publications Department, Anti-Defamation League of B'nai B'rith, 823 United Nations Plaza, New York, NY 10017.

Claudia's Caravan is a huge repository of multicultural and multilingual books, videos, records, games, and teaching materials. Its catalog is a real eye-opener to the wide range of materials available in the marketplace that kids can enjoy. Write to P.O. Box 1582, Alameda, CA 94501. Call 510-521-7871. Fax: 510-769-6230.

A catalog of books, dolls, and videos is available from Sensational

Beginnings, 300 Detroit Ave. #E, P.O. Box 2009, Monroe, MI 48161. Call 800-444-2147. Fax: 313-242-8278.

Heather Williams, the proprietor of Positive Images Children's Books, has gone the extra mile and written summaries of the multicultural books she carries. This is helpful in deciding which books are interesting and appropriate for your family. Visit her shop at 593A Macon St., Brooklyn, NY 11233, or call 718-453-1111.

These days it's hard to find a city with a substantial population that *doesn't* have a book or toy store devoted to multiculturalism. The few we list here all have catalogs and offer mail-order service:

The Black Earth, 476 Santa Clara Ave., Oakland, CA 94610, or call 415-465-4145.

Cadaco Company, 4300 W. 47th St., Chicago, IL 60632, or call 312-927-1500.

Chocolate Huggables, 317B Orange Rd., Montclair, NJ 07042, or call 201-744-5972.

Cynthia's Toys and Games, 501 14th St., Oakland, CA 94612, or call 415-464-3646.

Lomel Enterprises, P.O. Box 2452, Washington, DC 20013, or call 202-526-1196.

Colorful World, 2363 E. Stadium Blvd., Ann Arbor, MI 48104, or call 313-741-1177.

Looking for suitable and enjoyable videos? Call or write these companies for a listing of their tapes:

Coalition for Quality Children's Video, Santa Fe, NM. Call 800-331-6197.

"The Family Video Guide" by Terry and Catherine Catchpole. Call 800-234-8791.

CC Studios in Weston, CT, has a series called "Stories from the Black Tradition" and video versions of children's books by illustrator Ezra Jack Keats. Call 800-543-7843.

The Children's Television Workshop, producer of "Sesame Street" and other shows on PBS, has programs of "Reading Rainbow" on videocassette. Write to 1 Lincoln Plaza, New York, NY 10023, or call 212-595-3456. (In September 1992 a new CTW show, "Ghostwriter," made its debut on TV, featuring a multiracial cast of youngsters who try to solve mysteries.)

Specifically for adults is a documentary released in January 1992, *Color Adjustment,* directed by Marlon T. Riggs, covering the history of how African Americans have been represented on TV. It is now on tape, so ask for it at your local video store or library.

And if you need a little help in talking to your children about race or about sensitive issues in general, look into *How to Talk to Children About Really Important Things,* a book by child psychologist Charles Schaefer.

Parents and teachers should keep in mind that there are museums devoted to specific cultures, and, increasingly, larger museums are creating departments or carrying exhibits devoted to many cultures. One example is The Kid's Bridge at the Children's Museum of Boston (617-426-6500), designed to help youngsters appreciate diversity. Another example is the Museum of Tolerance, which opened in February 1993 in Los Angeles. This $50 million enterprise attempts to celebrate many cultures and stresses that people of diverse backgrounds can live together.

Specifically for educators and mental health professionals (and parents with a special interest in either field), useful texts are:

Race, Color and the Young Child, by John E. Williams and J. K. Morland (Ann Arbor, MI: Books on Demand, n.d.).

Coping with a Bigoted Parent, by Maryann Miller (New York: The Rosen Publishing Group, Inc., 1992).

Black Child, White Child, by Judith Porter (Cambridge, MA: Harvard University Press, 1971).

Children and Prejudice, by Frances Aboud (Cambridge, MA: Blackwell, 1988).

Counseling and Development in a Multicultural Society, by John A. Axelson (Pacific Grove, CA: Brooks/Cole Publishing Co., 1993).

Before the Mayflower: A History of the Negro in America, 1619–1964, by Lerone Bennett, Jr. (Chicago: Penguin, 1993).

Multicultural Counseling: Toward Ethnic and Cultural Relevancy in Human Encounters, by John M. Dillard (Chicago: Nelson-Hall, Inc., 1983).

On Teaching Minority Students: Problems and Strategies, by Gayle Pemberton.

Understanding Race, Ethnicity and Power: The Key to Efficacy in Clinical Practice, by Elaine Pinderhughes (New York: The Free Press, 1989).

Cool Pose: The Dilemmas of Black Manhood in America, by Richard Majors (New York: Touchstone Books, 1993).

Childhood: A Multicultural View, by Melvin Konner (New York: Little, Brown, 1991). Primarily photographs.

The Persistence of Racism in America, by Thomas Powell (Lanham, MA: Littlefield, Adams, 1993).

Race Matters, by Cornel West (Boston: Beacon Press, 1993).

Prejudice and Your Child, by Kenneth Clark (Hanover, NH: University Press of New England, 1988) and *The Nature of Prejudice,* by Gordon Allport (Reading, MA: Addison-Wesley, 1979). Though somewhat dated, these two books still offer profound insights.

Sage Publications, Inc., Newbury Park, CA, specializes in scholarly books, such as *Racism and Education, Promoting Cultural Diversity,* and *Bridging Differences,* on the many aspects of multiculturalism. For a catalog, call 805-499-9774. Fax: 805-499-0871.

Specific Sources

To keep this guide to a reasonable length, in this category we offer only a sampling of various materials. There are hundreds, perhaps thousands, of additional items available.

How do you find them? If research is not one of your strengths (as authors, we know how much "fun" it can be!), there are shortcuts: Order them from one of the general sources above (the catalog from Claudia's Caravan is an excellent starting point), ask your local public or school librarian, or inquire at a video or toy store. If the item cannot be immediately found, these people are usually quick to satisfy your inquiry. At the very least, requests from patrons and consumers indicate that a demand is growing for these materials, and it is more likely supply will increase to meet that demand.

And, again, please don't simply hand an item to your child. Use it together. Very few explorers go it alone. Shared knowledge is a personally enriching and memorable experience, one that lasts a lifetime in your child's mind.

BOOKS
(In order, from younger to older children.)

This Is My House, by Arthur Dorros (New York: Scholastic, 1992). Brings you into homes around the world.

Con Mi Hermano/With My Brother, by Eileen Roe (New York: Bradbury Press, 1991). About a young boy who admires his older brother.

The Legend of El Dorado, by Nancy Vanhaan (New York: Knopf, 1991). A story told by the Chibchas Indians of South America.

Ashanti to Zulu: African Traditions, by Margaret Musgrove (New York: Puffin, 1980). A Caldecott Medal winner.

Bringing the Rain to Kapiti Plain, by Verna Aardema (New York: Puffin, 1992). Based on an old Kenyan folktale.

All the Colors of the Race, by Arnold Adolf (New York: Beech Tree Books, 1992). A collection of poems expressing the inner feelings of a biracial child.

Colors Around Me, by Vivien Church (Chicago: Afro-Am, 1971). Discusses what the title indicates.

Bread, Bread, Bread, by Ann Morris (New York: Mulberry, 1993). A photographic tour of bread in many shapes and forms around the world.

Moon Was Tired of Walking on Air, by Natalia M. Belting (Boston: Houghton Mifflin, 1992). A collection of South American Indian folktales.

Darkness and the Butterfly, by Ann Grifalconi (Boston: Little, Brown, 1987). About a girl who understands and loses her fear of the dark.

Jambo Means Hello, by Muriel and Tom Feelings (New York: Puffin, 1985). Introduces some aspects of African culture. The Feelingses are also the authors of *Moja Means One: A Swahili Counting Book* New York: Penguin, 1987).

Mama, Do You Love Me? By Barbara M. Joosse (San Francisco: Chronicle, 1991). About an Inuit mother and child in Alaska.

People, by Peter Spier (New York: Doubleday, 1988). Takes readers around the world to show how each of us is a unique human being.

A Story, A Story, retold by Gail E. Haley (New York: Aladdin,

1988). Tells how the Anancy stories (remember the Raffi song?) got their names.

Families Are Different, by Nina Pellegrini (New York: Holiday House, 1991). About how families come in many shapes, colors, and sizes. There are over two dozen books in this series, from Aboriginal to Zulu.

Why Mosquitoes Buzz in People's Ears, by Verna Aardema (New York: Puffin, 1993). The rhythmic retelling of a West African folktale.

Amigo Means Friend, by Louise Everett (Mahwah, NJ: Troll 1988). The story of how a Spanish-speaking boy and an English-speaking boy learn each other's language.

Why Am I Different? by Norma Simon (Morton Grove, IL: Whitman, Albert, & Co., 1976). Addresses many of the fears children have about not being exactly like others.

A Place for Everyone, by Barbara Resch (Wilmington, DE: Atomium Books, 1991). A charming animal fable about looking different from the group yet finding acceptance.

Where Indians Live, by Nashone (Newcastle, CA: Sierra Oaks Pub. Co., 1989). A picture book that shows the diversity of American Indian dwellings.

Cornrows, by Camille Yarborough (New York: Sandcastle, 1992). About how two young girls learn about their hairstyles.

Angel Child, Dragon Child, by Michelle Surat (New York: Scholastic, 1989). Tells the story of a Vietnamese child's transition to life in the United States.

Any book by Ezra Jack Keats. His stories often feature youngsters of all colors in realistic settings.

In the Beginning: Creation Stories from Around the World, retold by Virginia Hamilton (New York: HBJ, 1991). Demonstrates that there are surprising similarities and imaginative differences between diverse cultures. Hamilton also retells traditional tales in *The People Could Fly: American Black Folktales* (New York: Knopf, 1993).

Lightning Inside You, edited by John Bierhorst (New York: Morrow, 1992). A collection of 140 riddles, word knots, and puzzles that demonstrate the wit and wisdom of Indian peoples from Alaska to Brazil.

Follow the Drinking Gourd, by Jeanette Winter (New York: Knopf, 1992). Based on folk songs sung by slaves in the American South.

Rachel Parker, Kindergarten Show-Off, by Ann Martin (New York:

Holiday House, 1992). About two girls of different races who look beyond skin color to become friends.

Feathers and Tails, retold by David Kherdian (New York: Philomel, 1992). Offers folktales from many cultures.

The Origin of Life on Earth, retold by David A. Anderson (Mount Airy, MD: Sights Productions, 1991). A lushly illustrated West African creation myth.

El Chino, by Allen Say (Boston: Houghton Mifflin, 1990). Features a Chinese boy teased because he wants to be a basketball player.

Brother Eagle, Sister Sky, by Susan Jeffers (New York: Dial, 1991). A romance about the environment, written from the Native American point of view.

Desmond Tutu: Bishop of Peace, by Carol Greene (Chicago: Children's Press, 1986). Chronicles the life of the South African Nobel Prize winner.

Martin Luther King, Jr.: The Story of a Dream, by June Behrens (Chicago: Children's Press, 1979). A play about the civil rights leader, with excellent illustrations, too.

Mummies Made in Egypt, by Aliki (New York: Trophy, 1985). Explores ancient Egyptian culture, which continues to influence that country's present culture.

Billy the Great, by Rosa Guy (New York: Delacorte Press, 1992). Tells the story of two sets of parents who are uncomfortable with the growing friendship between their young sons, one black and the other white.

Spinning Tales, Weaving Hope, edited by Ed Brody (Philadelphia: New Society Publishers, 1992). A collection of twenty-nine stories about living with ourselves, one another, and the earth.

Let Freedom Ring, by Myra Cohn Livingston (New York: Holiday House, 1992). About Martin Luther King, Jr., and includes lines from his most memorable speeches.

Hector Lives in the United States Now, by Joan Hewett (New York: Lippincott, 1990). About a Mexican American child who lives in Los Angeles.

Song of the Trees, by Mildred D. Taylor (New York: Bantam, 1984). A trilogy of stories, told by a girl about her family during the Depression in Mississippi, that involves prejudice, courage, and self-respect. Taylor has also written *Let the Circle Be Unbroken* (New York: Puffin, 1991) and *Roll of Thunder Hear My Cry* (New York: Puffin, 1991).

Iggie's House, by Judy Blume (Boston: G. K. Hall, 1989). A story about the prejudice a black family experiences when they move into a white neighborhood and the friendship that develops among the children.

Morning Girl, by Michael Dorris (New York: Hyperion, 1992). Set in 1492, this story is told by two Native American children, who witness the arrival of Columbus.

Black Folktales, retold by Julius Lester (New York: Grove Press, 1991). A good opportunity to read aloud to children stories of the African American experience.

Neighborhood Odes, by Gary Soto (New York: HBJ, 1992). A collection of twenty-one poems about a Mexican American community.

The Rough-Face Girl, by Rafe Martin (New York: Putnam, 1992). An American Indian variation of the Cinderella story.

A Million Fish . . . More or Less, by Patricia C. McKissack (New York: Knopf, 1992). A group of tall tales about black life in the Bayou region of the United States.

The Ancient One, by T. A. Barron (New York: Philomel, 1992). A fantasy story about a struggle between good and evil, based on Native American traditions.

Sounder, by William H. Armstrong (New York: HarperCollins, 1989). Winner of the Newbery Medal, this is the story of a black boy's search for his missing father and dog. If the book isn't readily available, rent the video.

An Indian Winter, by Russell Freedman (New York: Holiday House, 1992). A story of European explorers who are befriended by Native Americans.

Teaching and Learning in a Diverse World: Multicultural Eduation for Young Children, by Patricia G. Ramsey (New York: Teachers College, 1986). A look at multicultural education, accompanied by instructions on how to implement programs in school and social settings.

Winston-Derek Publishers (Pennywell Dr., P.O. Box 90883, Nashville, TN 37209; tel. 800-826-1888) offers beautifully illustrated books that retell traditional fairy tales from a black perspective, such as *Jamako and the Beanstalk, Beauty and the Beast, Sleeping Beauty,* and *The Ebony Duckling.*

We also want to point you to magazines devoted to children and children's issues that increasingly are addressing the need for understanding between racial groups and for raising unbiased youngsters. For example, one reason this book came into being was an article in the October 1990 issue of *Child* magazine, and this monthly publication has continued to deal with race-related topics. Other magazines to investigate (or write to the editor!) are *Parents, Family Life, Parenting,* and *Family Fun.*

VIDEOS

Adam's World: San Francisco follows a young boy in his multiethnic neighborhood ($29.95).

Beyond Tradition features Native American artists and their works ($35).

Big Bird in China shows our feathered friend discovering a culture on the other side of the globe ($24.95).

Ella Jenkins Live at the Smithsonian and *Ella Jenkins for the Family* have the popular folksinger performing for youngsters ($30 each).

Gung Hay Fat Choy captures the colors and excitement of Chinese New Year ($35).

Kwanzaa depicts a family celebrating the traditional African holiday ($37).

Koi and the Kola Nuts is about how an African tribal chieftain's son learns to have compassion for all creatures.

A Pair of Red Clogs is a Japanese story about the adventures of a little girl and her new footgear ($29.95).

Stories from the Black Tradition is a collection of five short films based on African and African American stories ($14.95).

Yo Estoy Aqui: I Am Here presents the experiences of a homesick child entering a foreign school ($29.95).

Inter Image Video specializes in African and African American entertainment and educational videos for adults and youngsters: Call 800-843-9448.

L&S Video Enterprises has a video series highlighting the work of black artists. Many museums have these tapes, but if you want your own copy (they retail for about $30), call 914-238-9366 or 212-841-0216.

Sensational Beginnings offers a variety of videos, such as *We All Have Tales* and *UNICEF Kids*, in addition to dolls. Call 800-444-2147.

Facets Multimedia in Chicago has recently issued an eight-hundred-title "African-American Catalogue" listing videotapes of films produced throughout the twentieth century that portray black life. Call 800-331-6197.

DOLLS, TOYS, GAMES, AND CRAFTS

Unless otherwise noted, the previously mentioned outlets, especially Claudia's Caravan, carry these and additional items, and they are described in more detail in the catalogs. Increasingly, department stores are carrying these items, but depending on where you live, mail order might be your best bet.

Ashanti, new from the Mattel Company, is a young African American girl waiting to be befriended. Other dolls from Mattel are Shani, Asha, and Nichelle.

Brown Sugar, Cherise, and Elise are dark-skinned dolls that are fun to cuddle and play with. For Brown Sugar: B 7 V Distributors Inc., P.O. Box 3854, Shawnee Mission, KS 66203. For Cherise, Elise, and Sun Man (a heroic black action figure): Olmec Corp., 7 W. 22 St., New York, NY 10010.

Classic Dolls and Marvel Dolls are playthings representing white, black, Latino, and Asian children. Ask for them at your toy or department store. Also ask for the new Kenya doll from Tyco.

Huggy Bean Dolls are a family of dolls with female and male infants, brothers and sisters, cousins and parents. The company has recently expanded its line into books, cassettes, and videos. Write to Golden Ribbon Playthings Inc., 1501 Broadway #400, New York, NY 10036, or call 800-722-8285.

Niños is a company in Michigan that offers cassettes and books on the Latino heritage as well as dolls and games. Call 800-634-3304.

African Inspirations in Landover, MD, has a variety of items for children and adults. Call 800-338-2365.

Keisha Doll provides more than forty dolls in a variety of skin tones, some based on historical figures. Write to Keisha Doll Co., 524 W. 174 St., New York, NY 10033.

Navajo Weaver Doll is made by Navajos and includes a loom with weaving, a woman, and a baby. A store that specializes in toys is your best bet. The same is true for Sangoma Dolls, traditional dolls made by Zulu mothers for their children.

The Pleasant Company makes baby dolls with a complete line of accessories in white, black, and Asian versions. Ask your toy store manager or call Pleasant Company directly: 608-836-4848.

B.T.'s Black Trivia ($25), from The Blakgame Group (P.O. Box 232, Brooklyn, NY 11233), is a fun game relating to black history. Another such game is Inner Vision ($25) from Inner Vision/Martha Hurse (P.O. Box 554, Mount Prospect, IL 60056).

Black History Playing Cards from Claudia's Caravan (see address above) contains fifty-two portraits of famous African Americans ($5.95).

Alerta is a manual of learning materials that in a fun way encourages children from different cultural backgrounds to learn about each other ($22.95).

All One People Buttons depict the earth from space with "All One People" written on buttons in twenty-three languages ($2 each).

Language Lotto is a game for up to eight players, accompanied by a bilingual cassette tape, with choices among several Asian languages ($11.95). A similar game is Loteria Mexicana, featuring illustrations of fifty-four traditional Mexican crafts ($9.95).

Poster Sets feature Asian, Native American, Latino, and African American personalities. Each set contains fourteen full-color posters ($9.95).

Where in the World? teaches, in a fun way, not only geography but the cultures of various cities and countries. It can be used by a family or an entire classroom ($35).

Art from Many Hands depicts arts and crafts from all over the world, according to continent ($14.95).

Children's World Atlas begins with a street map and expands to town, country, continent, planet, and solar system ($5.95).

Diversity in the Classroom shows ways to incorporate multicultural activities into the school environment ($11.95).

Grandmother's Path, Grandfather's Way is a rich collection of Hmong (Laos, Cambodia, Vietnam) folktales, that encourages children to create their own ($14.95).

Matsuri! is a collection of activities associated with Japanese American holidays ($9.95).

Multiethnic Studies in the Elementary Classroom has over two hundred pages of activities, including crafts, cooking, and holiday ideas ($25).

My Ancestors Are From . . . is a series of activity cards, each set of fifty-six to sixty-four cards depicting the heritage of one of over two dozen countries ($7.95 each).

Navajo Sandpainting Art has full-color illustrations and explanations of the symbolism ($5.95). Try your own!

Self-Esteem: A Classroom Affair has, in each of two volumes, over one hundred activities to help children work on enhancing self-esteem ($10.95 each).

MUSIC

Department, toy, and some record stores carry the following items. Another excellent outlet is Music for Little People, which has a beautifully illustrated catalog. To order a free catalog, call 800-727-2233.

All for Freedom contains songs celebrating African culture, performed by the American gospel group Sweet Honey in the Rock ($9.95).

American Indian Songs and Chants and *Walk in Beauty My Children* are tapes of folk songs performed by the Balem Sinem Choir, a Native American group ($9.95 each).

Canciones de Compañeros includes twenty-seven Hispanic folk songs in Spanish, with an English translation in an accompanying songbook ($15.95).

Children's Songs in Mandarin has ten versions of such favorites as "You Are My Sunshine" and "Skip To My Lou" ($10.95).

The House We Live In, two cassettes by the singer Nancy Raven, features children's songs from around the world ($9.95 each).

I Know the Colors in the Rainbow has Ella Jenkins and a children's choir taking youngsters on a musical journey through several cultures ($10.95).

Las Navidades is a collection of Latino Christmas songs in Spanish and English ($12.95).

Lullabies for Children will have youngsters heading for dreamland in Spanish and English ($12.95).

Proud to Be Cambodian has traditional songs sung in Khmer, with English translations in a booklet ($10.95).

The Singing Sack is a book of musical scores for twenty-eight songs from around the world to be sung aloud ($16.95).

Teaching Peace, by Red Grammer, promotes through music the theme of peace being an everyday reality ($9.95).

Earth Mother Lullabies, by Oamala Bellingham, is for very young children and contains soothing songs from many countries.

Even a selective resource guide demonstrates the vast wealth and range of material available to help children discover and appreciate cultural diversity. Whether you choose half a dozen or fifty items, or just one, we think you and your child will have fun and will begin to see the fabric of our society a little differently.

One request: After you and your child have enjoyed a resource, please be assertive about sharing it. Because of budget constraints or a lack of awareness, your local school might not have an adequate collection of multicultural books, videos, games, or music. Offer to bring a resource into the classroom or use it to fulfill one of your child's assignments, such as preparing a show-and-tell demonstration or an oral report. Offer items to your child's friends and their parents, play groups and day-care centers, and local organizations that involve youngsters.

At the very least, your child will observe that you care about what is being taught in your community as well as your home. We think you'll be amazed at the eager response from those who really do want to prepare children, and themselves, for a multicultural society, the Rainbow Generation.

Index